Gypsies & Travellers: A Teacher's Guide

STEVEN HORNE

Copyright © 2019 Steven Horne

All rights reserved. No part of this publication may be reproduced, distributed, or transmitted in any form or by any means, including photocopying, recording, or other electronic or mechanical methods, without the prior written permission of the publisher, except in the case of brief quotations embodied in critical reviews and certain other noncommercial uses permitted by copyright law.

Published by Amazon UK

Printed in Ridgmont, Bedford, England.

ISBN: 9781793076441

Steven Horne

To Woody (my cat), for sitting through 5 years of watching and listening to me complete my PhD. I'm pretty certain that you are now the UK's most educated cat, and probably the most bored. Thanks, little guy.

CONTENTS

INTRODUCTION 9

   A BIT ABOUT ME 9
   WHERE OUR JOURNEY BEGINS 11
   THE FIRST LECTURE 13

CHAPTER ONE: GYPSY, ROMA AND TRAVELLER HISTORY: A BRIEF INTRODUCTION 19

   GYPSY ORIGINS 21
   THE MOVE THROUGH EUROPE 26
   CONTEMPORARY HISTORY IN EUROPE 39
   SUMMARY 45

CHAPTER TWO: RELIGION, SPIRITUALITY, VALUES AND TABOOS 49

   RELIGION – A BRIEF INTRODUCTION 51
   RELIGION: SPIRITS AND SPIRITUALISM 56
   TRADITIONAL PRACTICE: MOKHHADI (OR 'THE PURITY CODE') 62
   SUMMARY 72

CHAPTER THREE: WHO AM I? 76

   INDIVIDUALS AND COMMUNITIES: PROVIDING AUTHENTIC INCLUSION . 78
   OLD HEAD, YOUNG SHOULDERS 81
   OLD HEAD, YOUNG SHOULDERS: MALES 84
   OLD HEAD, YOUNG SHOULDERS: FEMALES 88
   SUMMARY 90

CHAPTER FOUR: YOUR HEROES, STORIES AND LEGENDS, ARE NOT MINE 96

   STORYTELLING: A GYPSY ART 96
   KING HENRY VIII AND ANIMATED PRINCESSES 98

CHAPTER FIVE: BUILDING A RELATIONSHIP WITH THE STUDENT AND PARENTS 105

   FIRST THINGS FIRST 107

VISIBLE DIFFERENCES – INVISIBLE RECOGNITION 115
SUMMARY 121

CHAPTER SIX: COMMON QUESTIONS, STEREOTYPES, TERMS AND DEFINITIONS 123

COMMON QUESTIONS AND STEREOTYPES 124
COMMON TERMS AND DEFINITIONS 140
CONCLUDING REMARKS.. 142

BIBLIOGRAPHY 147

ABOUT THE AUTHOR.. 152

Steven Horne

INTRODUCTION

A bit about me

In 2010 I unknowingly changed my life forever. It was a sunny day in early spring, and I had just packed my 120th box of vitamin pills of the morning. Despite years of working and volunteering in multiple capacities, I had somehow ended up spending my days under the Dickensian-esque sheet iron roof of a pharmaceutical warehouse, in an attempt to earn a living. Don't get me wrong – I was eternally grateful for a regular wage and a (relatively) stable position. But I was incredibly unfulfilled. A series of stressful posts, including a stint in the Police, had left me feeling generally despondent and wanting an element of restful monotony in my daily life. Working a 9-5 in a warehouse therefore seemed to fit the bill. Until that day…

From out of nowhere and in a manner quite fitting of the spring day that our journey begins, a thought suddenly sprouted in my mind; "What am I doing with my life"? For clarity of position, this was a rhetorical question. Thanks brain. I put down the 'Mega Strength Vitamin C's and the Ashwaghanda (helps with bodily stress, in case you were wondering), and proceeded to speak to my boss, requesting to take a half-day's holiday. And with that, I left and headed directly to my local college. I never looked back. Within the next seven and-a-bit years I would earn: a Diploma; three more GCSE's; a 1st Class Honours Degree; a postgraduate certificate in Education; a fully-funded PhD Scholarship in Theology; and multiple awards. This seemed to be in direct contradiction to the stark diagnosis given to me by my D. T. teacher at Secondary school. Mr Rayner, who unbeknownst to me had taken a particular disliking towards me. One afternoon he summoned me to the front of the class, and proceeded to inform me of his position.

Perhaps it was because of my jumper that was too small or my hair that needed cutting? Perhaps it was because I was the smallest pupil in my class? Perhaps it was because I seemed uninterested in the work on the board? If only he'd realised that my single-parent mother did everything she could to present me well to the world each day, despite not having any money at all. If only he'd realised that my family's social-economic position meant that despite their best efforts, I was almost certainly underfed. We had no money, and very little food. Perhaps my teacher could at the very least give me some kindness?

Unfortunately in front of everyone, he proceeded to inform me (in a LOUD voice) that "you will never pass your

GCSE's, you will never get a job, you will never achieve success, and you will never amount to a thing". Thanks for the motivation and prep talk! Believing an opinion like that would unfortunately set me back on my life and work 'path' by around 10 years. Lesson One: *Your words hold unimaginable power, particularly towards those in your class living on the margins – figuratively and literally.*

Where our Journey Begins

I began my PhD in 2014, fresh off the back of my undergraduate dissertation that I had entitled '*What Gypsies and Travellers Believe and Why It Matters to the Church and Educational Providers*'. Ten thousand words later and all I was left with was questions and my own theories. Compared to my peers I felt inadequate. They had all devised pieces that offered grandiose conclusions and affirmative statements. Turns out questions are a good thing. I got offered a PhD Scholarship to go and find the answers.

I never knew back then that within a year of beginning my studies I would be standing in front of 180 trainee teachers, explaining as best as I could (within a very short time frame) certain intricacies of Gypsy, Roma, and Traveller (GRT) culture. The need and demand for clear and uncompromising information was shocking. Added to this dilemma were the time constraints that never allowed me to do the subject justice. Inclusion is important, but with the unyielding expectations upon new teachers and health professionals to be able to 'wear every hat', it would seem that compromise often trumps inclusion.

Every time I would conduct what was now an twice-yearly lecture, I would without fail receive numerous questions from people genuinely concerned with wanting to make a difference to those whom they taught and cared for. Those future teachers, along with many other professionals that I have instructed, had only ever seen a warped and often one-sided perspective of GRT culture. Most of the information and knowledge they held had come from TV programmes and media outlets. Further understanding had come from friends or relatives who seemingly only ever spoke of their negative encounters with Gypsies and Travellers. My lectures, which offered a fresh glance, seemed to hit them unexpectedly like a charismatic television preacher hitting his flock with a good old bolt of Holy Spirit. Bam! That imbalance of prior 'knowledge' that they all held needed to be addressed. This book attempts to address that imbalance by offering a brief and introductory glimpse into what is often an unknown and misunderstood culture.

The First Lecture

After a particularly challenging day of teaching I sat down with a cold drink, ready to continue watching (for the millionth time) one of my favourite TV shows – Game of Thrones. That particular episode featured Ygritte (Rose Leslie); a character from a people group known as the 'Wildlings'. Wildlings lived beyond the 'wall'; a physical barrier that marked the boundary between the civilised and the uncivilised, between those accepted and those despised. Centuries of mistrust and conflict had fuelled hatred, misconceptions, and ignorance. As a viewer, I was led to believe these myths concerning those beyond the wall.

But it was the unlikely romantic pairing of the lead character, Jon Snow (Kit Harrington) with Ygritte that began to shake this understanding. Working out of his prejudicial position, Jon is reprimanded by his new love with a now familiar statement – "You know nothing, Jon Snow". The statement, whilst contextually was meant for something else, got me thinking about my day. I had just delivered a lecture and workshop to the largest group I had ever instructed in one sitting. Nearly 180 trainee teachers were sat glaring at young man who appeared to be not much older than them, nervously trying to configure his PowerPoint whilst not coughing into the overtly sensitive microphone placed in front of him.

The students had been informed that I was going to be telling them how best to engage with Gypsy and Traveller pupils in schools and colleges. I was a last minute replacement after the University's previous speaker (a representative from the County's Council) had dropped out. Whilst I got ready, I couldn't help but notice their expressions and body language. It spoke volumes. They had already made their minds up. In that moment I changed the entire content of the lecture. It was either going to be the most stupid decision of my academic career thus far, or it would be fruitful. It was the latter, thankfully. At that point I had no idea that the lecture I had just delivered would birth a series of annual lectures and the book you are now reading.

Later in the day I would deliver a couple of workshops, serving as an extension of sorts from the lecture. I began the workshop by establishing what the trainee teachers knew (or thought they knew) about Gypsies, Travellers, and Gypsy culture in general. Whilst they remained respectful and professional at all times, the answers I received were shocking at best. I was faced with a generation that had an understanding of Gypsies and Travellers formed purely from mostly from 'big, fat' mass media sensationalism, tabloid press releases, and from entrenched stereotypes and prejudices. Many had not knowingly encountered or had interactions with Gypsies and Travellers, but nevertheless believed the hype.

In some ways I was shocked. Here before me were 180 critically-minded and inquisitive potential teachers, ready to provide influence and education to a generation of young people. Yet almost every one of them was operating out of a prejudicial and uniformed position. Sadly, I was not surprised. Hundreds of years of marginalising Gypsies had led to this point. Why would they think or understand any differently?

After listening to someone who had decades of experience and familial ties to the Gypsy community, they rapidly realised both their lack of knowledge concerning Gypsies and Travellers, and the potential for further social damage by continuing to operate out of their prejudices. I had metaphorically adopted the insider's position of Ygritte, and was telling these trainee teachers 'You know nothing, Jon Snow'! They were clever, they were challenging, and they were all amazing future teachers. But they were uninformed.

The combination of a miss-information from the larger 'settled' society and 'closed doors' from the Gypsy and Traveller communities had led to the position we find ourselves currently occupying. Beyond the safe boundaries of our comfortable existence lay the 'Edgelands'[1]; that uniquely metaphorical and tangible grey area of existence that occupies the space just beyond our

---

[1] Shoard, M. (2002).

own world view. In our minds it is the space where news of distant wars or famines reside; we know it's happening, we pull a sad face, say how terrible it is, and then carry on scrolling down our Facebook feed whilst drinking our spiced caramel latté (yes, I know they taste amazing). In our *real* world, the Edgelands is that disused car park with the temporary concrete bollards positioned at its entrance. It is the farthest part of the industrial estate that no one ventures to (other than HGV drivers slinging a bag of waste). And more often than not, it is that part of your town or city where the local Traveller's site can be found.

This book is intended to serve as a brief but crucial visit to these 'Edgelands' and the young people that reside there. Starting with a look into the history and origins of Gypsy collectives, the foundation is prepared for an unflinching exposé of Gypsy and Traveller culture, with a particular focus on the rationale and motivations of Gypsies and Travellers who are within the education system. It should also be known that this book is not intended to serve as a construct of apologetics. Its content is based upon years of objective research, interviews, investigations, and experience – both professional and personal. As such, it is my hope that this book be utilised as an assistant of sorts within periods of training concerned with inclusion and equality, or as a brief introductory guide for new and existing teachers, tutors, educators in general, and other professionals such as healthcare workers.

With that in mind, this book is designed so that it can easily be included in the development of both the experienced and the trainee professional educator – whether as a standalone recommendation or as part of an extensive training programme. As previously alluded to, there is much *we think we know* about Gypsy and Traveller culture, and much *we do not know*. For professionals with the public in our care, this is a dangerous concoction. Shakespeare quite aptly recognises this familiar and historic human position, stating that 'there is no darkness but ignorance'[2].

I still remember sitting in an undergraduate theology lecture at university. Someone suggested that a people group we were previously discussing "believe in the same weird stuff and act the same way as those Gypsies on the telly". "No they don't", I replied. "Okay then, what *do* Gypsies believe in then?" they asked. This book is my belated response.

---

[2] See Shakespeare's '*Twelfth Night*'.

Steven Horne

CHAPTER ONE: Gypsy, Roma and Traveller History: A Brief Introduction

In this chapter I will give a whistle-stop tour and necessary explanation of the foundations of Gypsy and Traveller history – a '101' if you like, of Gypsy, Roma and Traveller origins. I will also discuss elements of the history of the terms 'Gypsy' and 'Traveller', giving a brief explanation that will help you in addressing Gypsies and Travellers. This will help in understanding the particular nuances and preferences involved in the varying ascriptions chosen by Gypsies and Travellers, whether as communities, families or individuals. This in turn will also assisting you in confidently addressing misuse – or even potential racism in whatever environment you are situated.

Issues of racism or ethnical abuse when discussing Gypsies and Travellers may be an unfamiliar concept. However, a quick glance into GRT history reveals the tragic and unfortunate synonymous relationship between racialised mistreatment and GRT communities. Looking at this exposé of systemic abuse in some way contextualises the unfortunate disadvantage that many Gypsy and Traveller children have become accustomed to. As such, we begin this narrative where it all began. In doing so, an attempt is made to clear a pathway through which the rich tapestry of Gypsy and Traveller culture can be seen, devoid of media misrepresentation and uninformed accounts.

Quite often in life we can only make sense of the present if we understand our past. In reaching GRT children and their parents, it is important to have an understanding of both the culture and the reasons why and how the culture came to be. In many ways the history of the Gypsy is both inspiring and tragic. However, the notion that the victor always writes the history books has arguably never been so damaging. Negative portrayals and damaging stereotypes of Gypsies, which have been reinforced and encouraged by politicians, the Police, the media and the general population, is unfortunately not a new thing. Since their arrival to British shores, Gypsies have suffered exclusion, poverty, mistreatment and abuse on a scale not matched by any other minority group.

Finally, it is worth remembering that this is not an 'us and them' story; Gypsies have lived in the UK since the end of the 15th century. Generally this means that many Gypsies have a longer heritage and claim to the British Isles than those in the larger, more dominant 'non-Gypsy' society. Gypsy, or Traveller history, is in many ways the 'deleted scenes' section of some noble 'British establishment' movie, where the sins of the Commonwealth and visons of Empire creations are left to the wayside. Its relevance outside of the GRT community however, is found in the need to bridge cultural gaps and address citizens who are not 'they' or 'them', but 'us' and 'we'. Culture does not define nationalism, it defines a way of life. So for this history lesson, we are to learn and to understand the history of those of *us* who define and identify themselves as Gypsy, as Traveller, and as Roma. And in doing so, we may just begin to truly understand and see our society in its full spectrum of colour – rather than the basic black and white version we have been presented with.

Gypsy Origins

The modern Gypsy story begins in 10th century India. Whilst we do not have specific dates, we are able to develop reasonably accurate estimates based on our understandings of language. Linguistical experts in the field, such as Ian Hancock, have contributed immensely to a drive in preserving and making sense of what is at times a confusing language. But thanks to these efforts and others, we can accurately trace Gypsy origins back to India, where at some stage there was a mass exodus. Hancock dates the exodus to around the 10th century[3], whereas others date it much earlier[4]. Either way, the

---

[3] Hancock, I. (2001).

[4] Fraser, A. (1995).

exodus began in what we now know to be the state of Rajasthan, on the North-West side of India. The area was notoriously unstable and numerous factions and groups ruled the area.

At one stage, one of these factions – whom I shall refer to as Proto-Romani, was unsettled to the point that they were forced to leave their land. The Proto-Romani had no army, no Government, no land and no single ruler. Structurally they would have had 'leaders' per se, who would have represented and directed the collective in what would later become known as 'the Gypsy diaspora'. This structure of rule and leadership would persist for generations, with the leaders at some point becoming known as 'Gypsy Kings' – a title that is still used today amongst some groups and collectives of Gypsies around the world, usually as a term of endearment or for an individual who is greatly respected and known in his particular location.

The Roma (or Romani / Romany) would move eastward, through the Middle East, and then up into Europe. This is a passage way rather similar to the path used by migrants and refugees during Europe's 'refugee crisis' that has seen people from Syria being dispersed in their own modern-day diaspora (2012 – present day). For many, their journey would take a temporary stop in the bottleneck port-town of Modon (now known as *Methoni*)[5]. Modon was

---

[5] ibid. See pp. 51 – 55.

a small but significant trade point in Greece, and served as the gateway for trade and pilgrims to the Middle East and the Holy Land – Israel. As a result, the world's religions and cultures met in this single point as part of their individual journeys. The Roma, because of their vastly different appearance (bright and peculiar clothing, and a 'new' race), were ostracised from the beginning. Like many Gypsies and Travellers of today, the Roma were kept from staying in the central parts of the town, and were forced to the outskirts. At the time there were large hills by the town where the Roma temporarily resided, until invading Islamic forces (the Saracens) would once again unsettle them, forcing them northwards.

During their time in Modon, the Roma acquired two significant elements that would change their culture and perceptions forever. Firstly they acquired Christianity. Alongside their 'mystical' (or 'magical') practices, they began to blend in Christian values and beliefs, creating a new and unique presentation of the Christian faith. This trend of adopting cultural practices and beliefs became a trait of the Roma that would continue to the current day. In many ways this is no different to any other cultural, ethnic or racial minority that has struggled to survive, or had to deal with fleeing war or terror – without an army or political force of their own.

The second thing that the Roma acquired was a new name – 'Gypsy'. Whilst in Modon, the Roma, having to trade and deal with other traders and residents, would be noted for their vastly different appearance. Alongside this, their growing presence and settlement on the large hills of Modon were gaining unwanted attention and criticism. It was not long before they were referred to as a collective rather than as individual immigrants and refugees. Their dark skin drew a misguided association to Egypt – the nearest and most common trading point (where darker skinned people were coming from). As such, the Roma encampments on the outskirts of Modon became known as 'Little Egypt'; the residents thus becoming known as 'little Egyptians'. The Greek translation for Egyptian is 'Aigýptios', which would be abbreviated to 'gyptios' (pronounced 'Gyp-sos'). From here, 'Gypsos' would receive the Anglo Saxon treatment, eventually becoming the name and ascription – 'Gypsy'.

It is vital to recognise that the acquisition of Christianity and the collective name of 'Gypsy' are arguably two of the most pivotal junctures in Gypsy history. Evolving and embracing Christianity gave the Gypsies a real sense of identity in the process of developing a new people group from the wreckage of displacement and war. It would shape the entire Gypsy culture and outlook, and lead to remarkable modern-day statistics, such as over 80% of UK Gypsies and Travellers identifying as Christian. There were and still are Muslim Gypsies, with the vast majority currently residing in Eastern Europe. However, in comparison to the vast majority of Gypsies, the number of those affiliated with Islam is significantly smaller.

In adopting the term 'Gypsy', the Roma were willingly taking on a name that was born out of racial prejudice. There are good reasons for participating in this seemingly odd acquisition. Firstly, retrospective application of contemporary values is both impossible and unhelpful. In short, racism as we understand did not exist. By adopting the name 'Gypsy', the Roma were not conceding to racial oppression, but in a move that is arguably centuries ahead, were politically resisting such oppression. By reclaiming and repurposing the term, 'Gypsies' were being unified in their multifaceted struggles.

Secondly, by becoming affirmatively and collectively known as Gypsies, they became a recognised group, which in turn would facilitate recognition of individual communities. Also, as a collective they would be able to obtain goods, some rights, and possibly some form of power. Together they were able to identify as something, as someone, and perhaps more importantly – actually be recognised. Furthermore they were able to barter and to trade on behalf of *their* people, rather than struggle as individuals.

However, it is important to remember that the identifying name 'Gypsy' was born out of what we can now easily identify as a racist narrative. Thus the name and title

'Gypsy' has remained contentious ever since, with some individuals vehemently opposed to the term, whilst others being extremely proud to identify and call themselves Gypsy. The term 'Traveller' was a later development for a separate group within the GRT collective. As with 'Gypsy, this term was created from a perspective of observation (albeit minus the racist slant), due to 'Traveller' or 'Travelling' being an action rather than an unchangeable genetic feature. Note the usage of capital letters for Gypsy and Traveller; many publications – particularly newspapers often ignore this detail, resulting in the continued idea that Gypsies and Travellers are something or someone who is 'other', 'less than' etc.

Whilst I prefer to only use the term 'Traveller', it's important to recognise that there are still many people who prefer to identify as 'Gypsy'. If you are reading this book as a teacher or lecturer, you may find it useful to ask your Gypsy and Traveller students what they prefer to be recognised as; in doing so, you may avoid any potential pitfalls or assumed racial slurs or digs.

The Move through Europe

The transition from Greece to the UK would take around 2 - 300 years, with the first arrivals of Gypsies to British shores occurring in the late 15th century. It would be 1505 when the first Gypsy was 'registered' in Scotland, followed shortly afterwards in England. By the late 1520's CE the influx of Gypsies was increasing rapidly and by the end of the decade attitudes towards them from the settled population had changed for the worse. King Henry the VIII was in the process of reconstructing England's church as he saw fit, and removing any traces of 'superstition' and 'abuses' from the pulpit to the parishioners. Henry would take exception to the gradual influx of nomadic people arriving on British shores whom were reported operating as palm readers, fortune tellers and sorcerers; something that the church strongly opposed.

Henry's solution to the situation would come in the form of the *Egyptian Act 1530* which would officially deem it illegal to be a Gypsy in both identity and practice. The act would specifically target those who practised the 'crafty sciences' and those who were 'feigning knowledge in palmistry'. The Act also presented 'solutions' to deal with the Gypsies and presented those affected by the bill with limited options. The Gypsies who were charged were to either voluntarily leave the country within 16 days or face deportation; failure to abide by this ruling would result in the Gypsy's goods being confiscated and distributed to the local authorities, followed by the imprisonment of the Gypsy.

The rapid demonization of the Gypsy community developed as the reformation was gathering pace. Until this point, the Gypsies travelled with relative freedom through the various European states. In a series of alleged meetings between the aforementioned 'Gypsy Kings' and representatives of the Vatican, certain groups were given 'Papal' letters of protection. These letters authorised by the Pope ordered nation States to allow the Gypsies to travel through, and encouraged the giving of alms and shelter where possible. There were however limitations within these documents of passage, preventing the Gypsies from stopping in one place for an extended period of time. With some degree of haunting oddity, the past is once again incredibly representative of the present day!

However, given Henry's well-documented and problematic relationship with the Roman Catholic Church and the subsequent split from the Holy Roman Empire, it would appear to be of little surprise that the letters of protection that had served the Gypsies so well were now essentially worthless. It would seem highly improbable that Henry's predicament with Rome would alone have been reason enough for his hostilities towards the Gypsies, but their loss of protection afforded by Catholic documentation would not have helped in any way.

By 1554 the penalty for being a Gypsy who refused to leave the country had escalated to capital punishment. The move to execute 'Egyptians' had been an additional edit to an Act bought in during 1547 that enforced brandings and enslavement of 'master-less men' to prevent the Sojourners from settling in one place for too long. Philip and Mary, who now held the throne, defended their continued drive against the Gypsy population by using their 'Christian' voice and associated power to demonise the Egyptians, using Christianity as a measure against their ways; '[they (the Gypsies) use] their old accustomed devilish and naughty Practices and Devices, with such abominable Living as is not in any Christian Realm to be permitted…'[6].

By the 17th century, slavery had started to develop as a very real and pressing issue. The Gypsies had been experiencing restrictions of some sort for a while, as laws concerning personal freedoms for those who could claim no official residency and 'master-less men' had taken hold. The Church legitimised the use of slavery, and given the social and political status of the Gypsies, they stood little chance in avoiding losing their status as 'free' people. Nearly 150 years previously to this, Pope Nicholas V had issued a decree named 'Dum Diversas'; an act which actively encouraged and enabled slavery, and was essentially geographically limitless in terms of its application. Dum Diversas gave the following permissions:

> 'We grant you by these present documents, with our Apostolic Authority, full and free permission to invade, seek out, capture, and subjugate the Saracens,

---

[6] Fraser (1995), See p. 130; Keet-Black (2013), See p. 13.

pagans and any other unbelievers and enemies of Christ wherever they may be, as well as their kingdoms, duchies, counties, principalities, and other property and to reduce their persons into perpetual slavery'[7].

The initial stage of slavery for Gypsies came in the way of forced labour and an attachment of sorts to a master during the 16th century; by the turn of the 17th century it had developed into the traditionally understood 'chattel' slavery. For some of the Gypsies, they would become commodities in a system that was initially given its authority from the most senior elements in the church. It seems to be quite ironic that a people group who moved with such freedom and expressed a degree of faith and Christian affiliation would eventually be ostracised and enslaved by the very authority that it operated by and through. However, a change in legislation in the early 1700's stopped the deportation of native-born Gypsies; a move which potentially prevented another full-scale diaspora. The move was not entirely water-tight and there remained for some time a percentage of Gypsies sold into slavery and shipped back across Europe, as well as to the Caribbean and the Americas, where they would be sent to plantations in exactly the same manner as their African counterparts.

---

[7] Cameron, J. (2014).

The Reformation was beginning to create an environment of hostility and political segregation for the Gypsies in a way that attacked almost every part of their daily existence. From identity to travelling, begging and pilgrimage, Gypsies found no safe haven other than conformity to the state and a denial of self (as a Gypsy) and association with anybody else identifying themselves as Gypsy. The Catholic Church had for all intents and purposes turned its back on the Gypsies – and now the Protestant Church was actively doing the same.

Martin Luther had introduced a theology which had elements that would be later known as the 'Protestant work ethic', which in-part helped to change traditional approaches to the poor, as secularisation and the questionable spiritual value of almsgiving came into effect. Previous legislation such as the *Egyptian Act 1530* placed 'Egyptians' in the same category as beggars and vagabonds because of their methods of obtaining finances. As such, Gypsies were logically seen as 'poor' and thus treated the same as other people in the same social category. The developing humanist renaissance championed the tenets of success and activity. Poverty and laziness were subsequently seen as having an inseparable association with each other and provided grounds – both spiritually and socially, for rejection and condemnation.

Unfortunately for the ill-perceived Gypsies, the growing Protestant movement seemed to have agreed on common ground with the stereotypical understanding of Catholic thought concerned with *working for salvation*. However, it took the 'work ethic' element and primarily applied it to spiritual *development* rather than spiritual security. The downside to the change in attitude being that the Gypsies (as well as other 'poor' elements) saw a three-pronged attack from the Government, the church and the general populous. The option to leave the British Isles was not necessarily a wise choice as much of Europe was enforcing the same (if not harsher) restrictions and punishments on the 'idle wanderers'. The rise and divisions of nation states throughout Europe at that time, combined with the Reformation, saw religious freedom from Rome, and subsequently a 'strengthening [of] the authority of national monarchies vis-à-vis Rome'. This created a fundamental issue for the nations to define loyalty and belonging to both the State and to the church.

Loyalty and belonging to the church was defined by which denomination one identified with, i.e. Catholic or Protestant. This furthered the idea of identity and belonging to the State, causing even more identity issues for the Gypsies who were now the subjects of intense political suspicion and scrutiny, owing to their constant movement and lack of national identity. The Gypsy became a scapegoat for the political elite who used their war of denominational affiliations to oust those whom could not be defined so readily. Historian Becky Taylor highlights a particular incident where the Tudor state passed blame on the Gypsies for plots towards Elizabeth I and the harbouring of spies. The accusation of Gypsies themselves being spies soon developed and spread through Europe. This went so far as to seeing a law passed in Germany that would legally associate Gypsies with espionage. As a result, there was a severe limitation on the Gypsies' potential movements throughout the continent. That particular law reads as follows:

> 'When credible proof exists that they are scouts, traitors, spies and explore Christian countries for the benefit of the Turks and of other enemies of Christendom [it is] strictly forbidden to allow them to travel in or through their states to traffick, to give them safe conducts, escorts or passports'[8].

Once again, the combination of Christianity (or at least the usage of in name) and the ruling bodies offered no allowance or understanding for the Gypsy existence. In spite of this, Gypsies continued to practice Christianity and to develop their own religious fervour through worship and ritual. Evidence suggests that they continued to travel throughout the British Isles practicing Christianity relatively

---

[8] Taylor, B. (2014).

freely, with records evidencing the baptisms of Gypsy children as widely-spread as Suffolk and Devon.

The 18th century saw the introduction of an established and ruling parliament, which in turn meant that the Monarchy lost its authority. Consequently, the Church, with the head of state as its head, also gradually lost its distinct influence and power. The modern age with its secularised drive had arrived, and with it came a new and changing focus where productivity and the introduction of education would take centre-stage. All of this would have direct consequences for the Gypsies and Travellers who had managed to survive thus far.

The church would need to adapt to remain relevant and influential. In some ways it could be said that this new period where the church became politically less-significant enabled it to put more energies into its fundamental aspects of outreach, ministry and charity. An example could well be the State's introduction of an education system; the church in both Catholic and C of E guises took on-board the initiative and eventually began to produce many schools throughout England that were built on a strong Christian ethos. Perhaps more importantly, it was the church that recognised, or at least acknowledged the gaps in the demographic spectrum of school or educational institute attendees and sought to address the needs of those excluded by the state system.

The first elements of church-led education in the UK came by way of 'Sunday schools', which were focused at reaching the poorest in society. However, the church for the most part continued its hostilities towards Gypsies, refusing entry for educational activities and thus contributing to an environment that excluded Gypsies from all forms of public education. At some point there was a gradual change in attitude. Certain practices emanating out of London may have proved to be influential to other Churches and schools. News began to spread about Stockwell Chapel who were running a separate fully-functioning educational institute called 'St Patrick's Charity School'[9]. During the winter months the adjoining Chapel provided accommodation and education for Gypsies. It quickly became apparent that functioning in this manner enabled the Church educators to create a highly evangelistic environment.

As the educational system developed into a decidedly mainstream product, the secular sponsors and agencies gained a reasonable level of influence which hampered the Church's newly-found evangelical and ministerial drive towards Gypsies. The Church strangely responded by adopting the governmental position that saw Gypsies as a collective that were justifiably 'criticised, feared and scorned on any number of accounts', and were therefore

---

[9] Keet-Black (2013).

in need of reform and settling. This motion was actively and forcibly enforced by the magistrates and police.

In 1870 William Edward Forster introduced a revised version of the Education Bill in which Forster described schools in general as a defence 'against crime' and against other dangers to communities. This was a step-up from the Royal Commission who in 1858 had suggested that a school's moral influence was 'greater than their intellectual influence', or rather the 'gentling of the masses' as David Gass would prefer[10]. As the 20th century progressed the Church of England steadily lost their influence in education and subsequently the capacity to improve social function. Even critical voices such as Karl Marx and Friedrich Engels held a frustrated admiration for the influence and massive success of the 'gentling' or 'civilising' constituent of the Church of England's education vehicle[11].

The drive of education from the Church was perhaps undermined by political intent and decentralised by the underlying evangelical message accompanying the institutionalised instructions. Barring the actions of a few parishes and chapels such as the previously-mentioned Stockwell Chapel, there was an overall consensus that

---

[10] Cribb, A. & Gewirtz, S. (2009).

[11] Raines, J. (2002).

was in opposition to not only the Gypsies' *actions* but the Gypsies *themselves*. This failed to deter many Gypsies who continued to practice their conglomeration of spiritual practices and Christian traditions[12].

During the 19th century the London City Mission proved to be a highly vocal element within the Church of England that actively articulated their opposition towards the continued social difficulties faced by the Gypsy community. They instead provided and encouraged the uptake and participation in education, met basic welfare needs and also delivered the message of Christianity. Many Gypsies who partook in tarot card reading and other psychic phenomena for their own interests were said to have rejected such practices and adopted the counter-teachings of the church, with many reported to have gone on to become missionaries and evangelists.

The Gypsy community began to produce several key evangelical figures. They were to ignore the catholic rejection of the 'Little Egyptians' and begin preaching the gospel themselves. Arguably the most notable evangelical Traveller voice during this period was Rodney Smith. Rodney 'Gypsy' Smith (1860-1947) converted to Christianity in 1867 in Cambridge. He was largely self-educated and had an overwhelming desire to become a minister. Smith's 'calling' led him to the London City

---

[12] See *Chapter Two*.

Mission whereupon he was recruited by William Booth as an Evangelist with an 'outreach' organisation that would eventually be known as the Salvation Army. Smith spent many years on a global preaching spree that saw him settling in a modest Methodist community in Hull. Smith's influence and eventual stature resulted in a greater level of tolerance between the church and Gypsy communities on an international scale. Meanwhile, people such as Bartholomew Smith (Rodney's cousin) helped develop relations and improve social perceptions of Gypsies in the UK by joining forces with Thomas Barnardo through ministry and social activism.

The struggles faced by Gypsies in the British Isles during the latter part of the 19th century were predominantly centred on issues of adaption, owing to the Industrial Revolution changing almost every aspect of British society. Sporadic communities moved to larger towns and cities, forming new condensed urban areas. Traditional trades that Gypsies and Travellers had depended upon (producing goods for the purpose of hawking, repairing and tinkering), all declined as cheaper manufacturing meant replacing goods was as cost-effective – if not better than repair. Gypsies simply could not compete, and would have to innovate, as they always had done, in order to survive.

Contemporary History in Europe

The end of the 19th century and the dawn of the 20th saw a new wing of attack, in the amalgamated form of social philosophies and science. Unbeknownst to the creators, their ideas would later be used to justify atrocities against Gypsies. Science, as is understood in the contemporary sense was still in its infancy and as such, philosophical debate sometimes formed the basis upon which new scientific theories were developed. Arthur de Gobineau's *'Essai sur l'inégalité des races humaines'* (1853-5) created a notable influence on political and philosophical thought throughout Europe, particularly in Germany. The primary theme circulating through Gobineau's theory was that the decisive factor in historical development was down to race, and that there are 'lower' and 'higher' races in existence[13].

These theories of 'pure blooded races' would eventually be utilised by so-called 'Gypsiologists', who to support their own research, proposed the existence of a pure Gypsy race (or bloodline). The Gypsiologists' work was heavily romanticised, or in short – one-sided and heavily dependent upon stereotypes. Their work completely dismissed normal human patterns of relationships outside of primary community groups, and historical factors such

---

[13] Reilly, K., Kaufman, S. & Bodino, A. (2003). Also see; Fraser (1995).

as the diaspora and other collective movements. Unfortunately the seemingly supportive 'pure blooded Gypsy' narrative was adopted by many Gypsy and Traveller people. This would eventually be used as a method of maintaining separation between the larger settled populous and the smaller GRT collectives, resulting in terms such as 'Gorger' (a Romany word for non-Gypsy) and didikais (a Gypsy / Traveller of mixed parentage – one Gypsy, the other Gorger), as well as the maintenance of strict cultural codes (see *Chapter Two*).

In what would prove to be a history-altering move, Gobineau uses the term 'degenerate' when describing his ideas of what he sees as 'irreversible cultural decline'; a state where:

> 'a people has no longer the same intrinsic value as it had before, because it no longer has the same blood in its veins; continual adulterations having gradually affected the quality of the blood'.[14]

The philosophical debate concerning race and its aspects of superiority and inferiority was further developed by Cesare Lombroso's work 'L'uomo delinquent (1876), which exclaimed the notion of the atavistic origin of *criminal activity*[15]. In addition to this, the 'Social Darwinism'

---

[14] Moore, G. (2004).

[15] Duggan, C. (2006).

perspective gained massive popularity from around the turn of the century. Its message essentially suggested that a person's worth was based upon their usefulness in society, and that attention and encouragement should be given to the biologically beneficial parts of society – as opposed to protection of what could be considered lesser elements[16]. The application of these ideas concerning racial or cultural superiority partially operated as an ongoing response to concerns over the destruction of the slave trade. Meanwhile, these ideas of European origin were to be utilised to devastating effect much closer to home.

Germany, 1928. All Gypsies (Roma) were put under permanent Police surveillance. This followed the release of '*Anthropology of Europe*' by Professor Hans Gunther in which Gunther claimed that it was the Gypsies who brought foreign blood into Europe. Interestingly Gunther's work was dubbed as the 'Bible of Nazi Anthropology'. It would seem that the hijacking of Christian concepts to perpetuate the Nazi ideal had begun. 1930 saw the start of a 3-year legal process to introduce mandatory sterilisation of Gypsies, and by 1934 it was illegal for a German to marry a Gypsy. By 1936 there were 45,000+ Gypsies living in Germany, with almost all practicing what was considered 'traditional' Gypsy life. To Nazi eyes however,

---

[16] Wells, D. (1907).

the Gypsies were unhygienic and an antisocial nuisance that had to be dealt with.

Researchers were sent to investigate the Gypsies. Family trees, dwellings, locations, records of family names, ancestries and measurements of physical features such as nose width and length, cranium size and eye colour were taken. This same practice was also conducted on Jews, homosexuals, Blacks, and people with certain disabilities. All the records were put on file and lists were compiled of where everybody lived. As a result of this, the Gypsies were forced to sell their caravans and move into flats and other shared accommodation and then register officially with the State. Because of the research, the State knew everything there was to know about the Gypsies. There was no chance of escape or movement. From there the systematic movement of Gypsies from their homes to ghettos and labour camps began, and with that, the slaughter of around a million GRT people took place.

Post-war Britain saw the gradual introduction of various political moves designed to protect Gypsies and Travellers. The developments essentially outlawed things such as enforced slavery and exploitation, which surprisingly were still not illegal when applied to GRT people! However, the move can viewed with a certain degree of cynicism due to the distinct absence of Gypsies in slavery or specifically exploitative situations. As tragic as it was, the Nazi attempt at eradicating the Gypsies was not exploitative nor was it a move towards maintaining slavery. Slavery was indeed used, but as a means-to-an-end rather than the 'final solution' itself.

Colin Clark identifies the growing trend by the state that sought to regulate the everyday existence of the Gypsy[17]. Liberals and Humanistic elements began to argue that Gypsies and Travellers were 'adaptable' to social change and were now to be considered useful and therefore worthy of reintegration and assimilation; a process that Michael Stewart identified as 'proletarianization' – a process of the 'rigorous discipline of socialist labour'[18]. Rather than being directed specifically towards the Gypsies and Travellers themselves (and risking the potential for criticism), legislation began to emerge that placed restrictions and boundaries on where, when and for how long the general populous could stop or stay in certain areas. Such moves directly affected 'their [Gypsies] cultural norms and practices'[19].

This move towards legally writing Gypsies and Travellers out of existence through political means is continuing in the present day. During 2014, the British Government forwarded a recommendation to once again change the

---

[17] Clark & Greenfields (2006).

[18] Stewart, M. (1997).

[19] Clark & Greenfields (2006).

legal definition of what it meant to be a Gypsy or Traveller. In essence, it suggested that in order to be recognised as a Gypsy, one must be travelling for work or other purposes for 'X' amount of time per year. If this did not happen, then the State would no longer recognise that individual as a Gypsy or Traveller. The implication of this proposal was that someone's race and ethnicity was dependent upon an action, rather than a genetic, biological or historical factor. In 2016 this motion was approved; its implications are yet to be fully measured.

Beyond the purely political and religious, in the UK and the USA a new form of public hostility arose, in the form of sensationalist media. From anti-Gypsy tabloid newspaper headlines to social media hate campaigns, anti-Gypsy rhetoric was rife and seemingly ignored by any legal or moral bodies. Objectification of Gypsies came in multiple forms. From Hollywood movies to documentaries airing on established British television channels. Such documentaries also produced multiple spin-off programmes, including adapted versions that dealt exclusively with glamorised American Gypsies – as if they were a slightly different 'breed'. Such programmes had incredibly devastating effects (and still has) on Gypsy and Traveller communities around the UK.

To add to the frustrations of GRT communities that I have worked with, many non-GRT people have admitted to me that all they really know about Gypsies has come from such 'Big Fat' documentaries. This list of people includes many professionals in multiple sectors that I have personally encountered. They include but are not-limited-to: Councils; Government-led agencies; health professionals, and teachers (trainee and qualified). It would seem that these mostly fictional representations of GRT communities has continued the harmful myths and stories that have plagued Gypsies and Travellers throughout the centuries.

Summary

In a nutshell, the Gypsy and Traveller story unfolded in the following way:

Around 1000 CE, a large number of people were displaced from North-West India. The collective would be known as the Roma. The Roma would move west, eventually reaching Greece and fringe European states. They would begin to be known as 'Gypsies' and most would adopt Christianity. The 'Gypsies' would use the term 'Gypsy' as an identifier and as a symbol, and would use Christianity as a mode and model for living. The Gypsies made their way through Europe, gaining a (mostly) safe passage by way of letters of protection – issued by the Pope. Upon reaching British shores around 1500, Gypsies began working and contributing to British society.

Because of tensions between Henry VIII and the Catholic Church (over marriage and divorce issues), England would create its own Church – the Church of England. Henry VIII now had 'legal' rights to object to these 'Papal' letters, meaning that protection offered by the Church to Gypsies was no longer recognised by the State. Henry would make it illegal for people to identify or 'operate' as Gypsies. The reigns of Edward VI and Elizabeth I would see Gypsies faced with the threat of capital punishment.

After the death penalty was eventually removed, Gypsies were essentially downgraded to 'less-than'; a move that was later used to justify slavery against Black people. This of course meant that Gypsies were now a *commodity*, and could be traded, used and sold as property. This is one of the reasons for a Gypsy presence in America. In spite of a chequered history towards Gypsies, the Christian Church would eventually become a vehicle of equality and a voice for Travellers and Gypsies, offering freedom, education and health care during the Victorian period and beyond.

The secularisation of European culture and political power, along with key 'scientific' research, meant that legal protection for Gypsies began to rapidly disappear. The early 1930s saw Gypsies in Germany being physically measured, in a bid to know more about this 'sub-human'. By 1936, Gypsies were being moved to encampments, where they could be more effectively monitored. As a precursor of what was to come for the Jews, in 1938 they were being taken to the gas chambers. By the end of World War 2, around 1 million Gypsies had been murdered by the Nazis. Physical violence towards Gypsies and Travellers was frowned upon and less acceptable after WW2. This meant that European governments would have to resort to other means in order to deal with the 'Gypsy problem'. Legal motions that have seen Gypsy and Traveller ways of life made illegal, and media campaigns that have attempted to strip away cultural dignity, have all been used.

The result is a situation whereby the Gypsy and Traveller is ostracised, demonised and victimised. They are arguably the victims of the last 'acceptable racism', and suffer daily because of ingrained stereotypes held by many non-Gypsies. Whilst there are undoubtedly problems within some Gypsy and Traveller communities (as there are in many non-Gypsy communities), they are for the most part victims of circumstance.

Gypsies have the highest rates of male suicide; they are misunderstood in schools and educational facilities; their Christianity is 'unfamiliar' and therefore questioned; they receive poor standards of healthcare due to not being able to register with Doctor surgeries (due to moving around); they have the highest infant mortality rates; they have the lowest exam results rates and the highest school exclusion figures; they have the highest ratio of prisoners compared to every other ethnic and racial identity in England (including white males) at over 10% of all British prisoners being Gypsy or Traveller; and the average age of death for Gypsies and Travellers is the lowest in the UK by an average of at least 10 years.

GRT history is both tragic and awe-inspiring. It is one that speaks of enduring and overcoming suffering and insurmountable problems, but also one that highlights the dangers of unchallenged political, religious and secularised power. But reassuringly for Gypsies and Travellers, it is one that is yet to be completed. For Gypsies and Travellers, it is hugely important to remember the past, ancestry, and historical struggles. Through doing so, GRT people are empowered through an acute awareness of their personal and collective victories, of their endurance and adaptability, and of their rich heritage. If one is to secure a future, one must first know one's past. Sometimes this past is recounted through the art of 'storytelling' (see *Chapter Four*). At other times it is relived, reimagined, and repurposed through the explicit and implicit practice of religious and spiritualist performance. The significance of this historical contextualisation cannot be underestimated. As such, the following chapter will explore the fundamental area of religion and spirituality, along with their synergistic values and taboos.

CHAPTER TWO: Religion, Spirituality, Values and Taboos

"That's the third fire engine they've called today". A frustrated, tired and sleep-deprived groan coming from my host Lee – a Romany Gypsy from Southern England, as he began waving his arms at the approaching Fire and Rescue team approaching the Council-owned stopping site. "Sorry fellas, there's no issue here. It's the locals who've called again. We've had a funeral on". "No problem mate. We have to respond if there's a call though. You know how it is", replied one of the Fire crew. "Yeah, we know how it is". Lee's dour response a poignant reminder of the awareness that he had for both his and his community's 'position' in relation to the larger population.

The local Fire and Rescue service had been called several times due to a fire that had been burning on the site for nearly two days. Whether out of ignorance or genuine concern, other locals had called emergency services to investigate and eliminate the fire that in all fairness was relatively small in size and producing very little in the way of smoke and smell. If those who had reported the fire had taken the time to simply ask if everything was okay, or was to ponder a little longer why a group of men and some boys had remained by the fire's side for over 24 hours, they may have saved themselves the trouble of calling for

Fire and Rescue to arrive. But then this was yet another misinterpretation of a traditional practice (amongst many other quirks, nuances and traditions) undertaken by a number of Gypsy, Roma and Traveller people.

In this instance, Lee and his family had lost a close family member in unexpected circumstances. The funeral had taken place the day before, and as is tradition amongst some Gypsy and Traveller families, certain possessions of the deceased family member (such as soft furnishings, clothing and furniture) were being burnt. This was undertaken with the belief that the possessions go with the deceased person from this life into the next; this aides the spirit in the transition from one world to another. Smaller items, such as trinkets, money, photos and jewellery were also taken to the afterlife, but were transported with the deceased inside the coffin. Some families also choose to burn the trailer (caravan or 'vardo') that the dead person dwelt in, but this is increasingly uncommon, due to the economic value of reselling instead. There were many other elements surrounding this situation that effected other people, such as the sudden and prolonged absence of several children from school who lived on the site.

This chapter explores some of the beliefs, religious convictions, and upheld traditions that support so many of the fascinating, peculiar, intriguing and important customs practiced in many GRT communities. As with all other elements within this book, some of these beliefs and practices mentioned will not apply to some GRT groups, other groups may practice or believe a variant of what is mentioned, whereas others may not see or recognise these patterns or practices at all. It is a great time to remind ourselves that no single group can be entirely defined or collated within a single statement or text. And like many other cultures and ethnicities, GRT communities are comprised of many groups and many individuals, all with unique ways of conducting life. Collectively however, we can see a rich tapestry of convictions and important ideals. Whilst the focus still remains upon young people, the nature of exploring foundational religious ideas and concepts such as 'purity' means that this chapter will discuss these ideas and concepts broadly, and where applicable will provide relevant real-life examples.

Religion – A Brief Introduction

The religious beliefs and ascriptions to particular religions held by Roma, Gypsies and Travellers has irrevocably and undisputedly shaped and influenced GRT culture from its inception to the present day. Whilst there is no specific 'Gypsy' or 'Roma' religion per se, there is an overwhelming affiliation with Christianity by most Gypsies and Travellers. However, in certain parts of Eastern Europe, there are small pockets of Roma who identify as Muslim. The majority of Roma Muslims are found in Turkey, with many others residing in the Balkans. In terms of global percentages of religious affiliation (not including atheist or agnostic) within GRT collectives, Islam makes up just under 0.5%, whilst Christianity makes up nearly 99%. With particular reference to GRT communities in the UK, over 80% identify as Christian, 5% identify as non-practicing Christians, 6% identify as believing in God but with no particular religious affiliation, 6% identify as agnostic or atheist, with the remainder being unknown.

As for the nature of 'Gypsy Christianity' in the Western hemisphere, I propose that it is predominantly pluralistic in nature, meaning in this instance that the distinct and primary Christian core shares a stage with both spiritualist practices (obtained over the past 300 years) and implicit Hinduistic customs (obtained from its Indian origins). Roma religion finds its roots in its Indian origins, and this cultural ancestry still persists in everyday practice, although in a greatly reduced manner and a somewhat diluted form. These influences and practices manifest in certain practices and customs, and are discussed further throughout this chapter.

Certain TV programmes and media representations have greatly trivialised Gypsy and Traveller religious practices – such as weddings and infant baptisms, devaluing their importance and significance whilst simultaneously making such practices acceptable to public ridicule and shaming. Given the significantly high percentages of Gypsies and

Travellers identifying as or affiliating with Christianity, it is easy to see why the public mocking of GRT people undertaking Christian sacraments is harmful and damaging to both cultural relationships and community trust. Conversely, it is easy to see how using Christianity as a bridge or tool within classrooms is an effective and positive method for building relationships, gaining trust and encouraging class participation. And just to be clear, I am not suggesting that 'using Christianity' means evangelising and 'converting' your pupils! By all means, if you are Christian (or any other religion), then share the love! But inside the confines of the classroom, let's agree that the only thing we are going to convert are poor grades into better grades. What I am suggesting is that Christianity is a common denominator across multiple cultures and communities. This means that religious education lessons and Christian festivals (Christmas and Easter) are fantastic opportunities to develop overall class engagement and relatable content.

During many of the times I have delivered inclusion training to education and health professionals, a common assumption based on certain stereotypes often manifests that suggests the majority of Gypsies and Travellers are Catholic. There is some degree of truth in this belief, however, it is an evolving truth. Going back 500 years, early Gypsy communities made their way through Europe in relative safety due to Papal letters of protection. These were essentially letters issued from Rome (the home of Catholicism and the Pope), granting safe passage to Gypsies as they moved from one land to another[20]. During the Gypsy diaspora, the nationless Gypsies adopted the surrounding beliefs / religion, in-part as a form of cultural disguise, as well as a method of developing cultural identity. The adoption of the European-wide powerhouse that was Catholicism allowed them to survive as a collective. It wasn't until around 20 – 30 years after landing on British shores that the Catholic affiliation would lose its shine. This was partly owing to Henry VIII, his rather public divorce issue, and his subsequent founding of the Church of England (C of E) as a Protestant reaction to Catholic domination. The entrenchment of Catholic identity had been established, and despite a distinctly Protestant evangelistic push in the mid 1800's to save 'the heathen Gypsies'[21], for the most part many Gypsies (and subsequently, Travellers) remained as Catholic.

During the mid to late 20th century, a Church-based movement led by Gypsies began in France and eventually spread to the UK. It was an amalgamation of Pentecostal and Evangelical congregations and was led by and aimed towards nomadic cultures (Gypsy, Roma, Traveller, etc.). Its UK evolution would eventually give birth to the 'Light

---

[20] See *Chapter One*.

[21] Keet-Black, J. (2013).

and Life' Church. This represented a move towards Evangelical and Pentecostal worship for a growing number of GRT people. Whilst the majority of Christian Gypsies and Travellers still remain Catholic, approximately 35 – 40% now identify as Protestant – more specifically, Evangelical. I would argue that this denominational change, along with an evolution in work and income choices, are the two primary factors (amongst others) in the reduction of Spiritualist and 'superstitious' practices.

Finally, it must be said that there appears to be a distinct utilisation and absorption of religion amongst many Gypsies and Travellers, rather than authentic veneration and zealousness – in short, lip service. This does not negate in any way the genuineness of those who regularly worship, nor does it dismiss any validity in claims that Gypsies can and are God-fearing people. It simply suggests that religion can and often is 'used' for a plethora of reasons, rather than embraced and decoded with any degree of criticality or inspection; Traveller academic Damian Le Bas suggesting that 'proselytising and strident adherence to (Christian Church) creeds are not the norm'[22]. However, in recent decades the rapid increase in Evangelical and Pentecostal affiliation and worship is changing this characteristic.

---

[22] Le Bas, D. (2018).

Religion: Spirits and Spiritualism

Although there is a marked reduction in spiritualist/ism practices amongst many GRT communities in the current climate, there still remains elements. For the most part these 'superstitions' have evolved into different practices and subtleties. As an educator or services provider, you may encounter these practices and cultural patterns through indirect means. For example, the 'funeral fire' account given at the beginning of this chapter raises several issues that as a teacher, a tutor, a school, college or University, you may have to deal with. To begin with, there will almost certainly be a period of absence from the pupil / student. Whilst this is perfectly normal for any child dealing with a grief issue, you may find that the pupil stops attending school very suddenly and with little in the way of communication from the family.

Other factors around funerals may include being absent due to tiredness; sometimes the 'funeral fire' or another fire will be lit upon news of the loved one's passing. This fire will be attended to night and day by family (sometimes including children) until the deceased has been buried. Sometimes there are extended 'wakes' that can go on for days. Elements such as this will of course disrupt regular daily routines, but they should not be a cause of concern or worry.

Gypsies & Travellers: A Teacher's Guide

In some communities (usually Romany Gypsies) the deceased will be bought home the night before the funeral and kept in an open coffin. Surrounding the coffin will be candles to guide the way for the spirit to the afterlife and to prevent malevolent spirits from entering into the world of the living. All of the family will be expected to pay their respects to the deceased, including children. Having an open casket with the deceased in the same home as the family has been practiced by many people for time immemorial. However, it has become less common in the present day. As such, it might be worth keeping in mind that your pupil / student has just seen and spent time with a dead body for an extended period of time. Again, this is a very normal practice for many different people groups around the world and can help tremendously in the mourning process. But we live in a very 'protected' and sheltered country, where death is generally a hidden thing, an avoided subject, and a taboo conversation. So it may be worth spending some time with your pupil to let them talk if they wish, or to simply support them as a school, college or university.

The belief in malevolent spirits (as mentioned above) should not be trivialised. Likewise it should not be confused with age-old stereotypes concerning Gypsy psychics, palm readers and clairvoyants. It is true that there are a number of psychics etc. within the community, who work at fairs, circuses, and other temporary events.

However, for the most part this is more to do with the historic marginalisation of GRT people and the subsequent inability to access more streams of permanent and skilled employment. As a people group, some Gypsies and Travellers turned to delivering psychic services as a means of income. This practice has since carried on for several hundred years. Whilst many both within and outside of the community look at it as a bit of harmless fun, some take it a little more serious.

In both my recent fieldwork and within a number of historic accounts, there are some Gypsies and Travellers who support their loved ones who undertake such work, but will insist on it never being used amongst other GRT people. Amongst these accounts, people have reported a deep fear of 'opening doors' to the spirit realm. Therefore avoiding contacting the dead – particularly in one's own home, is a priority. This is one reason why psychic services such as palm reading and crystal ball gazing are often conducted within small tents – rather than fixed accommodation; home 'pollution' is avoided, and the 'portal' is closed every time the tent is dismantled. Mirrors are sometimes understood to serve as a similar 'portal'. As such, mirrors are sometimes covered up or turned to face the wall inside homes when a funeral is on and the deceased is being kept there.

Another element of spiritualism within the community is a strong belief in luck – good and bad. Occasionally this is linked somehow to the individual's Christian beliefs, but more often than not, it is part of a culturally inherited belief system. Many 'Old wives' tales' and 'lucky practices' originate from Gypsy sources, such as placing a silver coin in a cork and giving it to the groom on his wedding day for good luck and lasting happiness. There is a great aversion to the number 13 (considered highly unlucky). During a key period of field research, I never came across a plot no.13 on any official Gypsy and Traveller sites. On one particular site there were 20 plots – all had trailers (caravans) on them, except for plot 13, which did not display a number, but had the site's main sanitation facilities on it, along with some storage and waste containers.

There are other more common elements of 'luck' that many people outside of GRT communities are familiar with, such as the selling of 'lucky heather'. As with the psychic services, selling lucky heather (commonly seen in the high streets of towns up and down the country) has historically been a trade born out of necessity, with very little in the way of a traditional belief in the actual luckiness of the heather itself. It is a practice almost exclusively undertaken by females; most often those struggling financially. The 'luckiness' in this regard is not conventional, but harks back to the Roma Indian / Hinduistic routes, whereby luck is an element of karma. So essentially the belief translated into contemporary language reads something like this: By buying the small piece of lucky heather (often wrapped in silver foil), you will receive good luck, good fortune or a blessing, because you have blessed the seller of the heather, who is in need of money. In some larger gatherings, such as the world famous 'Appleby Horse Fair' (in the north of England), this practice has evolved into the selling of 'lucky' beads and charms – usually small brightly coloured glass and plastic pretty stones.

Other examples of lucky and unlucky practices / beliefs can sometimes be related to the use of language. On several occasions I have met family units who have unfortunately lost someone to a terminal illness, or had a family member who was currently dealing with an illness or health concern. Within these unrelated families there was an almost universal avoidance of particular terms – such as the term 'cancer' or the names of several age-related diseases. In each instance I carefully raised my awareness of their avoidance of certain words. I was told that it was unlucky to mention such terms, and to do so could increase someone's chances of getting that affliction. Other examples include the use of people's names after they have died but before they are buried. Mentioning the deceased's name can cause unrest, and potentially anger the spirit. This rule also applies to misusing a deceased person's name at any time after the funeral, or particularly if someone makes an attempt at contacting that deceased person via a Medium / Clairvoyant. Importantly, this latter 'rule' is also supported by Biblical instruction[23], where God warns both about the practice and the consequences of separation from Him for a 'defiling act'[24].

The inclusion of God within the equation of 'luck' brings our attention to the direct link between spiritual issues and karmic concepts, and subsequently the most common application of these. This takes the form of the Holy Spirit. The Holy Spirit, which is understood to be part of the God-head[25], is the spirit of God, and is believed to be present in every living thing. The Holy Spirit is believed to both respond to prayer / requests, as well as acting as an independent and constant force of change, protection and guidance in the background. Some Gypsies and Travellers also believe that they can pray to their deceased loved ones, who can operate in a similar fashion by either acting directly for the living or by passing on requests to God directly; this is sometimes known as 'intercession'.

---

[23] "Do not defile yourselves by turning to mediums or to those who consult the spirits of the dead. I am the LORD your God" (Leviticus 19:31 – Bible; NLT).

[24] "If a person turns to mediums and necromancers, whoring after them, I will set my face against that person and will cut him off from among his people" (Leviticus 20:6 – Bible; NKJV).

[25] Research 'the Holy Trinity' for a brief explanation.

This is just a brief introduction to GRT religion and spirituality. The aforementioned elements should assist in contextualising certain behavioural patterns and in starting meaningful and insightful conversations. After all, the best person who can tell you about themselves is often the person standing right in front of you. But sometimes there are exceptions to this rule. Within many GRT communities there are certain topics or even words that cannot or should not be discussed. And likewise, there are certain practices, behaviours and values that are not condoned. The next section shall begin a short exploration into what these topics, practices and values might look like, and the framework in which they reside.

Traditional Practice: Mokhhadi (or 'The Purity Code')

There are many ways of passing on traditions, ideas, belief systems or particular practices from one generation to another. All cultures to some extent do this. It is a phenomenon with explicit and apparent results. Yet categorising it and/or describing such a process is notoriously tricky. I once asked a number of individuals in an undergraduate class of mine to describe their culture to me and to explain how they learnt their cultural values. Most gave suggestions such as 'tolerance', 'democratic', 'supportive of arts' and other qualities that all sounded rather positive. I proposed that they had just described France and Holland, rather than England. At first they giggled, before looking a little dejected. National identity was challenging enough to describe, yet alone their individual and familial belief systems and structures. The same challenge is not only present amongst GRT people, but is arguably even more difficult. This is owing to the nature of how cultural values and practices (and conversely, taboos) are disseminated from one generation to another in Gypsy and Traveller communities.

Historically, GRT groups have passed on skills, values and collective behaviours through observed and repeated practice, demonstration, discussion and storytelling. Collectively this is known as 'oral culture'. Since their inception, GRT groups have mostly operated as an oral collective. This in itself has caused (and continues to cause) several issues. One consequence is that there are almost no historic documents produced by GRT people, meaning that a vast amount of GRT history (recent and old) has been documented and/or created by people outside of the community. Another consequence is that because certain trades are passed onto following generations by on-the-job training (usually at a young age), there isn't always an apparent need to enter secondary, further or higher education. This factor in particular when coupled with poor access to schools for nomadic Gypsies and Travellers, contributes to the ongoing issue of high illiteracy rates amongst some GRT people. But beyond these issues dwells a series of values, ideals, and practices that have shaped and directed entire GRT communities, and in many ways still do. Collectively they form something I shall call 'the purity code'.

Now to be clear from the outset, the purity code is not a mysterious element or tangible construct. Interestingly, it isn't something that is really spoken about, and it isn't something that has ever really been given a name. So having established what the purity code *is not*, let's establish *what it is*. Firstly, knowingly or unknowingly it is something that has been practiced by Gypsies, Roma and Travellers all over the world – sometimes explicitly, more often than not implicitly. The concept is located in the Indian-Romani term 'Mokhhadi', meaning *ritually unclean / ritual purity*. Technically there is no correct spelling of the term, owing to the developmental and oral nature of the Romani language[26]. In England, the term occasionally used is 'Chikli', which is possibly linked to the large Indian town of *Chikhli* in the Western region of India where the Roma diaspora is believed to have begun. The idea of 'Mokhhadi' – or *pollution*, was originally drawn from Hindu

---

[26] 'Romani' is the language used by Roma and some Romany Gypsies. It has developed and evolved over many centuries. Many GRT people who use Romani do so either as a secondary language, or by simply using particular Romani terms or words.

traditions[27] [28], although its manner of application in Gypsy and Traveller households has been likened to that found in orthodox Jewish homes[29]. As new generations emerge, fewer Gypsies and Travellers undertake some of the more traditional practices. Historically these practices would have included aspects such as males and females washing in separate basins.

The Mokhhadi phenomenon operates in a twofold manner. It is both a methodical practice, intended to maintain health (physical, mental, spiritual) and order (social, familial, religious). It is also a spiritual practice that incorporates superstitious beliefs and practices, as well as liturgical actions (Christian rituals, etc.). There is a belief that time spent in non-GRT environments can have a draining effect upon spiritual energy. Conversely, this negative effect can be reversed by spending time in an all-Gypsy environment[30]. It is in this environment and context of 'spiritual and physical wellbeing that the Indian origin of... [Gypsy] people is most clearly seen'[31]. The physical aspect focuses on a number of rules. These rules take

---

[27] Dawson, R. (2000). See pp. 3 & 9.

[28] Hancock, I. (2013). See p. 75.

[29] Clark, C. & Greenfields, M. (2006). See p. 41.

[30] Hancock, I. (2013). See p. 75.

[31] ibid. See p. 75.

numerous forms, and deal with elements of daily life. Typically these rules can include (but are not limited to):

- Water and waste separation
- The cleaning of clothes and bed linen / towels
- Preparation of food and drinks
- Washing and general hygiene / appearance
- Menstruating and childbirth
- Interaction with animals
- Cleanliness of the home environment
- Separation of males and females at particular times (such as at weddings and social environments)[32]

When the living quarters for an entire family is sometimes permanently located in a trailer, everyday cleanliness is of paramount importance. As such, thoughts and ideas on 'pollution' will often (in the first instance) adopt a practical appearance. For example, the toilet that is found in most caravans (or 'trailers'), are almost always never used by Travellers, owing to concerns about hygiene. Often

---

[32] Clark, C. & Greenfields, M. (2006). See pp.23 & 41 – 42; Keet-Black, J. (2013). See p. 20.

Gypsies or Travellers will remove the toilet and/or use the space for extra storage.

In stark opposition to the above information, there are common derogatory stereotypes that suggest 'Gypsies and Travellers are dirty'. During extensive field research into the practical application of Mokhhadi, Robert Dawson refutes such stereotypes. Instead he claims that in almost every instance of his case studies, the caravans (trailers) and their immediate surroundings were 'spotless'[33]. Furthermore, there is research that has been conducted by the Cardiff Law School (CLS) that supports Dawson's claims. CLS propose that less than 3% of Gypsies and Travellers are responsible for excessive waste and rubbish being left on the outskirts of camps and on illegal settlements[34].

Mokhhadi – or the Purity Code, can also be understood as a series of opposing or non-compatible elements. In this way, it becomes easier to define what is 'Gypsy' and what is not. This in turn makes it easier to establish and distinguish between what is acceptable and tolerable, and what is unacceptable and taboo. The unwritten purity code defines what is polluting and what is 'clean', but it is rarely non-negotiable. For example, many people believe there

---

[33] Dawson, R. (2000). See p. 12.

[34] ibid. See p. 12.

exists an element of separation between the Traveller community and the non-Traveller community. There is some truth to this, in that a number of Gypsies and Travellers would not choose to live as some settled people live. Furthermore, by maintaining a separation between cultures, there a remains a form of cultural protection from a larger society that would prefer a greater degree of integration.

However, it is a common myth that the two cultures are mutually exclusive from one another. Gypsies and Travellers have depended upon the larger society for work and financial opportunities for many centuries. Conversely and consequently, this means that the larger settled populous has also depended upon a degree of trade and work with GRT communities and individuals. So any degree of cultural separation should not be seen as an act of hostility, but understood as a form of cultural maintenance.

The theme of separation continues within Gypsy and Traveller communities. Traditionally this could be primarily observed between males and females; with examples mostly located within the realms of heterosexual relationships. Homosexuality and issues surrounding transgenderism amongst Gypsy and Traveller communities have generally at times been seen as taboo, as 'polluting', and as something generally frowned upon and unacceptable. It would be easy to propose the cause for these attitudes were down to traditionally conservative and deeply evangelical applications of Christianity, but this is merely speculation. It must be remembered that collectively British (and indeed Western) values and understandings concerning gay and trans issues have only been received more positively in recent decades, with gay and trans people still facing many hostilities and hate crimes in *all* sectors and communities of the UK.

However, within many GRT communities, attitudes and acceptance has and is changing. There are gay GRT activist groups and public figures within the community promoting issues of equality in public spheres. This may be worth remembering if any of your GRT pupils or students come out as gay or seek support in any of these areas, as there may be a chance they do not necessarily have any form of support network. This is a great reminder that GRT pupils are facing the same issues and pressures that any other young people are experiencing! Their support should be no different, but your awareness of potential issues should be enhanced.

On the theme of relationships, sexual intercourse before marriage is usually seen as both polluting and as something akin to a non-Traveller / non-Gypsy lifestyle choice. Dawson suggests that these approaches to daily living are not in retaliation to non-Gypsy people. Instead, Dawson proposes that such approaches are legitimate and relevant to Gypsies in maintaining both separateness and respectability between Gypsies and non-Gypsies:

> 'Even in these days of far more sexual equality, many of these taboos still occur, though the details differ slightly from family to family. Gorgers (non-Gypsies / non-Travellers) should understand that such practices, whilst not according with some modern ideas of gender correctness, are legitimate to the people who undertake them. The Gypsy sees the lack of such standards amongst gorgers as something quite shocking, and certainly illustrative of the gorger's degenerative state. This extends into the whole range of moral issues too, where gorgers are often seen as people who have low standards, care little for their elderly, break marriage commitments, are of easy virtue and corrupt'[35].

This statement by Dawson highlights how Mokhhadi as a cultural idea is something that evolves and isn't static. It can go from being a form of reasoning with just physical consequences, to something that invokes moral corruptibility from actions that are deemed to be questionable. In the classroom, this could be something as simple as a lesson on sexual health or relationships. As *Chapter Four* will highlight – what may seem acceptable

---

[35] ibid. See p. 10.

and normative in the classroom, may in fact be conflictual with one or more cultures.

One example of Mokhhadi potentially affecting class activities could be an interaction that a student teacher shared with me. The teacher was conducting a Physical Education (P. E) lesson, and were informed by a young Gypsy boy that he had forgotten his gym shorts. "Okay. Well you'll have to use a spare pair from the lost and found box". To this request, the boy got angry, refused, and started crying. He wasn't given the chance to explain why, and was reprimanded by the teacher for his behaviour. "I just couldn't reason with him", she explained. The student teacher went on to explain that this had happened more than once. Upon the third time of it happening, the school feared that the child did not have any shorts and that the family were possibly struggling financially. They asked the parents if they could give the boy some new shorts. "Are they sealed in a packet?" asked the mother. "Urm, yes" replied the teacher. "Then fine, he can have them. Thank you, that's very kind", replied the mother. In this instance, for the boy to have worn someone else's shorts – in particular, shorts previously worn by a gorger (non-Gypsy), would have been a polluting act.

Two important things can be learnt from this example. Firstly, that incidents such as these are, as Dawson alludes to, not an act of division or hostility towards non-GRT people but a form of cultural preservation and learned values. Secondly, there is no explicit expression or immediately obvious indication of a cultural code or 'act of pollution' etc. These terms simply help us to signpost and understand collective values and beliefs that might assist in developing more authentic and effective relationships – and thus inclusion. By being aware of the possible existence of these nuances amongst your own GRT pupils, certain challenges – such as the boy with the P. E shorts, can be better navigated.

Summary

There can be no denying the impact that religion has had upon GRT culture and communities. Religion, more specifically – Christianity, has historically been adopted by the overwhelming majority of GRT people and utilised in a plethora of ways. This inherent religious narrative has both created and ran alongside elements of spiritualism and spiritualist practices – sometimes in the form of superstitions, sometimes as sayings and phrases, and sometimes as cultural ritual – both practiced and avoided. The combination of these factors – religion and spiritualism, has at times caused confusion and conflict amongst some outside of GRT communities – most notably certain religious bodies and governmental offices. The trickledown result has been the problematic and divisive creation of stereotypes and excluding behaviours, such as assuming many Gypsies are or know Palm readers, or that 'Gypsies are dirty', or Gypsies and Travellers don't like education. By avoiding or dismissing the importance and centrality of religion and spirituality amongst GRT communities, many unhelpful stereotypes are allowed to continue.

At the time of writing this chapter, I along with many others were able to see the true nature of many Gypsy and Traveller communities, which is more often than not in direct contrast with such negative stereotypes. Each year there are a number of Gypsy and Traveller religious groups who actively respond to charitable issues. In recent years, these have been displayed on social media so that others both inside and outside of the community may donate and assist in some way. This year, thanks to 'live streaming', many people were able to see the generosity of 23 Traveller men arriving at a well-known toy shop brand in the UK, ready to make an enormous purchase of toys for local children's charities. Having spent over £10,000 on toys and children's gifts, they travelled to a number of charities to deliver the donations. It should be noted that whilst in the toy store, someone unknown called the police, because of their alarm owing to the presence of Gypsies / Travellers in the shop! Shortly before this campaign of kindness, another Traveller started an online 'nomination' challenge campaign, asking Gypsies and Travellers to 'fill a trolley' and donate the goods to their local food bank. The challenge was a huge success and went viral, spreading across the whole of the UK.

Unsurprisingly, neither campaign made the news or press. This is potentially owing to a persistent narrative within elements of the British press concerning the beliefs and behaviours of Gypsies and Travellers. By responding with an open mind and a desire for objective understanding, you as a professional – be it an educator, health professional or otherwise, can begin to undo these ingrained beliefs amongst those outside of GRT communities. Furthermore, such efforts will make an enormous difference to both the life chances of the young person before you and to communal cohesion amongst the many and varying collectives in the UK.

This chapter has helped to develop a broader picture of the historical foundations of particular cultural beliefs and religious preferences unique to GRT communities, and has looked at a few examples of certain nuances and cultural narratives, such as 'the purity code' and ritualistic behaviours at funerals. The following chapters will sharpen the focus towards individuals, with a specifically emphasis on young people. We will examine several key themes that focus primarily on beliefs held about oneself and one's community. These beliefs will be contextualised in relation to the past, the present and the future. As a professional, understanding these areas will provide you with valuable insights that could facilitate particular lessons, curriculum changes, interventions, general cultural awareness, and further conversation.

CHAPTER THREE: Who am I?

There are a number of studies that have attempted to either understand or explain both the challenges and/or nuances of teaching and connecting with young Gypsy and Traveller people. The majority of such studies are extremely helpful in developing a fuller picture of the landscape of GRT educational issues and factors. However, unintended issues can arise from such studies that unwittingly prevent substantial impact on both the lives of GRT individuals and on educational and social policy.

The first issue is that an overwhelming number of these academic materials are produced by non-Gypsies / non-Travellers. Whilst many of these works are culturally beneficial, they can damage the potential for authenticity. A common complaint from the GRT community that myself and other academics have experienced is that 'identity' (amongst other themes) in GRT groups is often investigated for the purposes of academic advancement, yet very little social action is ever subsequently undertaken. As such, a second issue arises as a consequence of the absence of authenticity. That issue is a lack of genuine cultural understanding about the young people who are often the subjects of such studies. In reaction to this unhelpful phenomena, this chapter will present an initial narrative on how young people in GRT communities are often understood and socially positioned. Such information serves as a backdrop and contextualisation to the previous chapter (2), '*Religion, Spirituality, Values and Taboos*'.

Starting such discussions has, in my experience, often been met by non-GRT people with raised eyebrows and burrowing deep down into seats, as people are taken out of their comfort zones and presented with language they thought they'd never hear inside University walls and terms they thought were inappropriate or offensive. The stark reality in these situations is that to achieve social impact, one must be socially impactful. This isn't a case of being offensive or explicit for no good reason, but more a situation whereby a softened approach to difficult situations – such as discussing criminality in Traveller and Gypsy communities, has become one item on an extensive list of 'no-go areas'. This trend for avoiding offence is prevalent in many areas of the Western world, in particular the UK and the US.

Whilst the method of protecting vulnerable communities and people by altering our language is for the most part both necessary and right, it can have the adverse effect of limiting discussion. This limitation, which is present in some non-GRT productions, limits both the impact and authenticity (as discussed above), which in turn limits both the understanding and any subsequent response by professionals, such as teachers, health professionals, and local councils. The next section gives an example of where such limitations have real-world consequences, and how we might respond. In doing so, we can both increase genuine inclusivity and have a greater understanding of who our young GRT pupils are.

Individuals and Communities: Providing Authentic Inclusion

A room full of curious, concerned and excited faces, all vying with one another to ask the next question. The topic: 'Gypsy, Roma and Traveller inclusion'. The students sat around me were all undergraduate trainee teachers, halfway through their degrees and ready for their next placement. Most had encountered Gypsy and Traveller pupils during their time spent in schools, but all were unsure as to what approach was appropriate in interacting with or responding to GRT pupil / parent concerns and behaviours. All of them wanted to be the best they could for those they had responsibility for. But no thanks to a rapidly developing social climate of cultural and personable offence sweeping University campuses and areas of employment, many were 'walking on egg shells' around collectives such as GRT pupils, or conversely they were ignoring the needs of GRT pupils entirely as they had received no instruction that GRT pupils were a recognised minority.

In these situations there is a dangerous, detrimental and paradoxical side-effect from either being overtly cautious with the language and approaches we use during interactions with marginalised and ostracised groups and individuals, or from ignoring cultural and personable differences and preferences. That side-effect is the eradication of genuine, quality and impactful relationships. How so? Both approaches forgo authentic human contact by entering the person-to-person relationship on terms of both the expectation and assumption of what that person or group wants and needs, or the dismissal of the existence of such needs entirely. What results is a toxic and somewhat familiar class scenario, whereby individualism is sacrificed for the collective identity of the class; meanwhile, pupils are simultaneously singled out as SEN (Special Educational Needs), as PP (Pupil Premium), as EAL (English as an Additional Language), or as a marginalised collective (for example, Jehovah Witness, Gypsy, Muslim). This action results in pupils being collectively assigned as 'other' or 'less than'; a far cry from any initial intentions of inclusivity.

One solution is of course a more holistic approach, whereby the teacher or professional is able to form meaningful relationships with each of their pupils.

Unfortunately time allowances, workloads, class sizes, and red tape means that pursuing greater interaction with pupils and their parents is not always possible.

However, pursuing a middle pathway whereby the individuality of people is recognised as a primary component in the formation of a stable, productive and positive collective, is a testable and reliable method of inclusion and recognition. I call this accommodating approach the 'village method', where classes are seen as micro communities – each with its own talents, abilities, and identities. In this way, 'class' (in the economic sense) is removed from the classroom, as is differentiation of ability, race, ethnicity, religion and cultural identity. Instead, these areas are celebrated and understood as crucial aspects of the collective identity of the classroom, school and indeed the local community.

Given the aforementioned restraints that slow or restrain the development of meaningful relationships (i.e. time allowances and class sizes), 'toolkits' should be adopted to assist in the process of gaining authentic and quality understanding of the individual collectives within classes, such as religious minorities and in this instance – GRT pupils and families. The content of these proposed toolkits would ideally include brief-but-critical materials of insight (such as this book), visits from local community leaders, and staff development sessions led by professionals (such as the lecture / seminar I referred to at the start of this section). All of the above recommendations could be implemented at any point within the academic year, and would ideally form part of ITT (Initial Teacher Training). This chapter reflects the concerned position of my students from the opening example of this section, and responds to the proposed solutions that I suggest – building deeper relationships and providing informed insights. It does this by taking a brief but closer look at the GRT pupils, asking the question 'Who am I?'. In doing so, the previous chapters are contextualised, and a clearer picture of the present-day condition of many GRT communities is given some light.

Old Head, Young Shoulders

Anyone involved in teaching – be it at a school, college, university or elsewhere, understands the crucial importance of knowing the abilities and barriers of the students sat before them. The increase of mixed-ability classes has raised the demand upon teachers to provide broader and more dynamic lesson plans, with a typical pattern consisting of base-level work for some, and further questions / tasks for those with greater abilities. Of course, these plans are based in-part upon the expectation of a shared and common vocabulary; not just a vocabulary built upon a common and shared academic pathway, but also a social vocabulary that finds its centre in an expected or assumed social environment. So what happens when that vocabulary encounters a different vocabulary? Or to put it another way; what happens when one culture meets another? Whilst working with a number of schools in London, it became apparent that such an event most commonly occurred with pupils whose primary language was not English. The expected response was unanimous – assimilation.

Whilst assimilation in this context was more often than not undertaken with care and usually with some awareness of cultural sensitivities, the message was clear: *English will become your primary language and British values will become your values*. Of course, this is both entirely understandable and ultimately necessary, if the pupils and their families are to have the best opportunities for overall wellbeing and acceptance as new residents within the UK. However, what happens when the dynamic is shifted, and the 'external' pupil and/or family have historically had their culture and community threatened by the host – or larger community / culture? In the instance of many GRT families and communities, the notion of assimilation is unthinkable for a number of reasons; not least because assimilating with the threatening host brings with it the possibility that one's own culture may come to an end. As such, I would propose that in the instance of facilitating marginalised, ostracised and minority groups / individuals, that *accommodation* is given preference over *assimilation*. This would apply to issues of race, sexuality, religion and ethnicity, to name but a few.

Accommodation provides a space in which we can safely contextualise our past, our present, our values and our beliefs – all whilst simultaneously (and safely) learning from and contributing to the larger or dominant host. This factor is crucial when working with GRT children and families, and is vital in the process of understanding other communities and cultures that may be alien from your own experience. With that in mind, we are positioned to look more closely at how young GRT individuals are understood.

To do so, we have to begin with what may appear to be a leftfield question: *When is a child not a child?* The age of criminal responsibility in the UK starts at 10 years of age, whereas the age of legal responsibility (marriage, paying tax, driving, etc.) can start as low as 16. However, we can all recognise that these legal and lawful binding structures do very little in terms of recognising individual ability, cognition, and social awareness. Let's take for example a 14 year old child that acts as their single-parent's carer. Their understanding and familiarity with a plethora of issues including finances, health, inequality, and independence, positions them as someone who is essentially a 'young adult'. In this instance their unfortunate external predicament has in many ways advanced their years. Compare this with a typical (if there is such a thing) upbringing of a child / teenager. We can quickly establish that assumptions made on the basis that all young people operate within a similar vein are both narrow and unhelpful.

This damaging method of interpretation is magnified when applied to GRT young people. There are a number of complexities at play within GRT communities – some explicit, many implicit. Without the proper contextualisation, many behaviours, approaches and attitudes may be grossly misunderstood. These complexities can broadly be placed within just a few categories. These categories include but are not-limited-to: age; gender; and sexuality. In the following sections (that are divided where necessary, i.e. males from females), notice how these tropes explicitly interplay with common GRT communal narratives, such as 'purity'[36], family and personal honour, and communal expectations.

Old Head, Young Shoulders: Males

An important transitional event happens with males in many GRT communities that affects how males interact with others and how they wish to be interacted with. The change in communal understanding of males upon

---

[36] See *Chapter Two*.

reaching around 12 years of age[37] is often noticeable in a sudden lack of attendance to Secondary education. This is commonly perceived by non-Gypsies to be a lack of interest by Travellers / Gypsies with education beyond basic instruction, i.e. that which is provided within a Primary education setting. Whilst there has historically been some truth in that statement, it is the internal social understanding of the community that has ultimately dictated his new path. At around 12 years, the male has transitioned from being a boy to being a man. With that change comes many new expectations and requirements. Whilst such a change may seem strange and arguably out of place within the contemporary UK (and Europe), it is in fact a practice that has occurred for millennia in multiple ethnicities and communities around the world.

This change is not sudden. Over a period of years, the boy is in many ways being prepared for his imminent responsibilities and new role. A high degree of social freedom combined with a considerable amount of time spent with adult males conditions the child to engage in ways that are at times surprisingly helpful, and other times potentially confrontational. A Gypsy boy that is familiar with patriarchal and heteronormative power structures may be fantastic when asked to serve as a captain for a school

---

[37] This is approximate and varies with different families / communities. Sometimes reaching puberty – rather than a particular age, is the deciding factor.

team, but might become argumentative when challenged over something he deems trivial by a female member of staff. This should not be confused as a deliberate act of sexist behaviour. Power, authority, community and familial roles are often very specific and assumed within GRT environments. People are often expected to fulfil certain roles and perform (or not perform) certain tasks based on variables such as age, gender, and physical abilities. Some of these 'traditions' date back to early Roma days (or even proto-Roma) when GRT communities were mostly nomadic, whilst others were acquired during the late 19th and early 20th century. The nature of being a vulnerable community travelling through the middle-east and Europe meant that issues of protection, hygiene, and general survival necessitated the aforementioned variables being applied to various roles. Communal survival is still a priority for many GRT people, albeit in an evolved manner.

Within the UK there are not any formal proceedings to mark the transition from boy to man. However, the new 'man' will often become more involved in the family line of work, meaning that in some families formal state education will make way for a *practical* 'Gypsy' education. Whilst many young Travellers and Gypsies will not be forced into work at such an age, social pressures and conformity become deciding factors. In addition, the lure of a wage at such a young age is also another incentive. For those that do stay in state education (even on a low attendance basis), their relationships with those around them (teachers, class assistants, and other staff) will now take on a new dynamic. The boy will now see himself in many ways as an equal to the adults around him. Whilst boundaries will honoured, the boy (now a 'man') will expect a degree of respect. Not for any unwarranted reason, but simply in the context that he is an 'adult' like those around him. As with all adolescents (GRT and non-GRT), there will be natural contentions, as the young adult attempts to understand their place in the world. It is worth remembering at such moments the additional difficulties and pressures that the Gypsy / Traveller boy could be contending with.

Evidence shows that many schools are aware of the potential for absence from Gypsy and Traveller children around this time – particularly for those pupils of an age who will be sitting SATS exams[38]. Schools will often refuse to take on new GRT pupils during such periods out of a fear that the lower abilities of the GRT pupils (due to nomadism and poor attendance) will reduce the overall school's scoring. As such, a perfect storm is created for the unassuming GRT boy. In addition to internal cultural factors drawing the boy away from a future Secondary education, there are also political and educational factors

---

[38] Cudworth, D. (2008).

pushing the boy from Primary education. Awareness of this unfolding dynamic is therefore key at every stage of the educational process.

Old Head, Young Shoulders: Females

For many young girls the fairy tale fantasy of marrying Prince Charming at a Disney-esque wedding is both common and harmless fantasy. For some young Traveller or Gypsy girls however, such a fantasy is located within a degree of tangible and expected outcome. No, the girl will probably not be marrying Prince Charming, but like many Disney Princesses, the girl will most likely be marrying young and marrying for life. A number of Gypsy and Traveller girls have unknowingly preparing for married life from a very early age. This would have happened through common channels, such as creative play, role play, and art. However, observation of and conversation with siblings and peers often forms the strongest foundations of the tradition of early marriage within GRT communities.

For those who are to become young brides-to-be, they will often be married at the earliest opportunity, which in the UK means exchanging vows as early as 16 years of age. Whilst many 16 year old's are contemplating both their GCSE's and their options for College / Sixth Form, some

Gypsies & Travellers: A Teacher's Guide

Gypsy and Traveller girls may be selecting their wedding dress or first home.

With the prospect of marriage comes other inevitabilities; most notably, having children. Consequently, this means that the 10 year old girl standing in front of you could be both married and a mother within six years. Due to some cultural sensitivities concerning sexuality (and discussions thereof), the biggest challenge found in this area is often found when going beyond the surface-level conversation of *becoming* a parent to discussing *how* one becomes a parent. In previous research that I have undertaken, I encountered 11 year old girl whose mother had only ever responded to questions concerning procreation by telling her that babies are delivered! When I questioned the mother further, she revealed that her tale consisted of something akin the story of the Stork delivering babies from the air in swaddling. She explained that she was 'protecting' her daughters from impure conversations and thought. It should be noted that although I encountered similar reports, they were for the most part quite rare.

In terms of this hyper-conservative approach to sexual issues, in some communities there are explicit examples of this transitional process from girl into womanhood. As the girl enters adolescence, some Gypsy / Traveller girls will begin to grow their hair out. Often the hair will left to reach the girl's waist or beyond. This will signify that the girl is both fertile and potentially looking for a partner.

Conservative values will mean that sexual contact in any form (sometimes even kissing) will be forbidden till the day of marriage. Hair can remain a factor beyond marriage. After the marriage, the woman may style her hair how she pleases, as long as it is not cut too short. After the lady reaches an older age (or the menopause), she will often cut her hair in a shorter style. This later trend is replicated in many other cultures.

Summary

And so a trend of transition – of nomadicy, is seen not just within the physical habits of certain GRT communities, but also within GRT ideology. There is an intentional movement from childhood into adulthood, with the security and future of the GRT ethnicity in mind. The consequence of this means that whilst play and fun as a child is supported, childhood is arguably a temporary luxury. From the outset, a percentage of Gypsy and Traveller children are conditioned for a life beyond that which they are currently experiencing. For males, a process of becoming a 'man' entails learning from and observing the men in his community, whilst simultaneously finding his place amongst his peers. His concern is not just with his multifaceted educational path, but with holding rank amongst his own. Education in this sense has a very different definition to the one that many around him might possess.

The struggle for educators thus becomes a two-headed beast. On one hand educators and service providers must provide relevance and engagement in what it is they are teaching or delivering at the time. And on the other hand they must actively prove the benefits of continual learning specifically within an educational environment. Such provision must be non-threatening and ideally applicable to the GRT individual's familial set-up. This can be partially achieved by asking questions such as: Are they semi-nomadic? Do they live on a site or are they settled? Do they live in town or are they pitched up on the outskirts of town? From there, one can begin to get personal and make content relevant. For example:

In your class you have Billy, a 9 year old Traveller. Billy hates his maths lessons and causes a distraction every time those number games come out of the class cupboard. Your task is to get Billy on side. How? By making it relevant. Billy's dad is a Landscape Gardener; a profession that Billy is almost certain to go into. So you ask Billy, "Billy, how much do you quote a customer for preparing and putting turf in their garden"? Billy tells you he can't give a price because he doesn't know the size of the garden. A fantastic opportunity has now arisen to teach Billy how to work out areas. From there you can take it further. "Billy, how much does the turf cost you"? Billy will know that his dad has to buy turf in rolls; each roll covers a certain area. Now we get to use more maths skills. Finally, we could get Billy to prepare a basic invoice for the customer with the details of price and area included. This reveals another issue; Billy has poor literacy abilities. Statistically GRT pupils have scored lower on particular school-based tests – especially those focused on literacy skills, in comparison to other minorities. But like every issue, a problem is not a problem – it is an opportunity to develop. Billy previously was not engaged in his English lessons. However, Billy is now invested in his task, as he wants to learn and earn!

As we've established, there are some distinct ideas in play concerning gender and gender roles. This most likely has you positioned in one of two thought processes. Some people may think 'these are old gender stereotypes and I will not support them'. Others may be thinking 'this is how Gypsies and Travellers think, and I will support them in their choices'. Here's the punchline – both thought processes are right and wrong. As educators, your primary job is to help people learn and develop. But we all know this is achieved in-part by expanding what we already know (or think we know). By showing GRT pupils options beyond the boundaries of what is familiar to them, you are providing them with an equal education and an opportunity for growth. Equally so, by also respecting their cultural choices and understanding that what works for you doesn't always work for someone else, you are allowing a spirit of multiculturalism to flourish within the safe confines of a respectful and recognised institution. This is inclusion.

It is vitally important to remember these principles when engaging with younger females (*see section above), as the temptation to impart personal values upon what may seem to be outdated cultural trends might be too great. Besides which, there is currently a cultural revolution within GRT youth. This revolution is creating a generation of young Gypsy and Traveller females who are politically and educationally engaged. In previous research I interviewed two females (15 and 16 years old). Despite generations of their relatives following the same path as each other, both girls were succeeding in their studies and were planning out their futures. One intended to go to University and study Law, whilst the other was preparing an application to attend her local college with the intention of owning and running a salon. Babies and marriage were a distant thought at best.

The point here is that as educators and service providers, you have an incredible opportunity to influence a young person's life – not just in the immediate sense, but in the distant future also. You also have an equally incredible opportunity to provide genuine support to someone who most likely does not receive support from any other external agencies.

Some of the alternative approaches to life choices mentioned throughout this chapter are built upon a combination of centuries of compounded belief patterns, and of external pressures and situations. The result is a set of cultural values that are passed down to subsequent generations by both oral and implicit means. It is not your job to change or question these values. But as the passage above alludes to, GRT and non-GRT cultures are not always mutually exclusive and many young Gypsies and Travellers have great aspirations to be academically successful. Many cultural values and beliefs in Gypsy and Traveller communities are present elsewhere, and many will be familiar. However, as this book has so far revealed, certain values, beliefs, and practices are exercised or performed in ways either contrary to popular culture or markedly different. The result can be confusing for those outside of GRT communities, which may then unfortunately be perceived as intolerance or disinterest amongst some GRT individuals. This disinterest – or conflict of interests, can sometimes manifest in the classroom or professional practice, presenting itself as an alternative social narrative. The following chapter presents a couple of insightful examples into some of the elements explanations that form these differing social narratives.

Gypsies & Travellers: A Teacher's Guide

CHAPTER FOUR: Your Heroes, Stories and Legends, are not Mine

Storytelling: A Gypsy Art

Many years ago, one particular cultural identifying trait of Gypsies was the apparently great storytelling skills displayed by some GRT people. There was an element of romanticist stereotyping present by picturing Gypsy communities as vibrant and secretive communities wherein stories and folklore thrived. However, in this instance there was (and to some degree still is) a degree of truth within the tales. Whilst there are many reasons for this, there are two factors which broadly explain this subtle-but-important element within aspects of GRT culture. Both factors are explicitly linked to the previously mentioned 'oral nature' of GRT communities, whereby information and learning is passed on or disseminated through demonstration, repetition, and/or verbal explanation.

The first factor was a response to the *external* world. To explain oneself or one's community, particularly when the first Roma / Gypsy groups were moving through Europe, verbal interaction was utilised rather than manifestos or policy arrangements. In recent decades, this has significantly changed, as many GRT-led activist and political groups have formed, delivering information on behalf of Gypsy / Traveller communities in a plethora of platforms to local, national and even European Councils.

The second factor was a necessary response to the *internal* world – Gypsy and Traveller communities and culture. Storytelling could be considered a normal and regular activity for many families and peoples – not just GRT people, to share tales and stories of past events or ancestors. However, it was and arguably still is a crucial aspect in the formation and maintenance of GRT cultural identity amongst many Gypsies and Travellers.

Further to this, there is another historical phenomena that has taken place through the development of these tales and stories. The exaggeration and 'filling in' of additional (perhaps not exactly historically accurate) details in certain tales, resulted in the creation of *folktales*. Many popular folktales, particularly in British culture, have at times seen their creation credited to Gypsies and Travellers. Whether such folktales originated in GRT circles or not is neither provable nor contestable. But this is where the nexus of Gypsy storytelling is located.

Understanding this broad and culturally-historic trait will help to provide some contextualisation when you, as a teacher or other professional present a history lesson, an assumed cultural truth, or a particular belief or stance. This is because these platforms of delivering and sharing information are sometimes used differently – or hold a different value to some GRT people. The following section highlights examples of both historical and modern Western themes (including popular culture), where this is the case.

King Henry VIII and Animated Princesses

Cast your mind back to the previous chapters, and you may recall that Henry VIII had a particular political influence over the new and expanding Gypsy population. As such, to illustrate this next point, we shall look towards the historical narrative of Henry VIII.

There are two aspects that should be noted when looking at King Henry. In the immediate sense, the first aspect is the details within the account of Henry, the years that followed and the subsequent impact upon Gypsy communities. Beyond that is the second aspect, where, in this instance 'British' culture does not result in the same conclusions for all groups and minorities that identify as British (or whatever the State identity is).

The Tudor period is often a popular subject to explore at school, more so at Primary age (Infant / Junior schools). Focus is usually drawn to Henry VIII at some point, who is often remembered by employing a common mnemonic device. Thus Henry's consorts and their particular fates are with some humour listed as "Divorced, beheaded, died, divorced, beheaded, survived". This often gets a smile from the class who have not only managed to remember a whole lot of history in just six words, but they've also just enjoyed the gory side of education, in what is essentially a 'Horrible Histories'[39] esque lesson. Henry VIII is never usually painted as a nice guy, but given the typical nature of how such lessons are presented, it is easy to dismiss, forget or even be entirely unaware of the devastating impact that Henry had upon the ancestors of any GRT young people in your class.

Henry would initiate a chain of events that would be supported and developed by other monarchs. The result was the imprisonment and deportation of Gypsies for the 'crime' of being a Gypsy. Gypsies were given the chance to renounce their 'Gypsy-hood', or face the consequences.

Eventually under different leadership this punishment would escalate to becoming a capital offence. Whilst this escalation did not endure for too long, Gypsies would not escape unscathed. Borrowing from over 300 years of European example and legislation, Gypsies became re-

---

[39] 'Horrible Histories' is a successful children's television programme (made by the BBC), which presents historical stories in a humorous fashion, specialising in emphasising the gory and disgusting side of true accounts.

categorised within the same social positioning as 'vagrants, beggars and thieves'. This meant that over a period of time, Gypsies lost their status as free and equal human beings, effectively forcing many into unpaid servitude – i.e. slavery. The newly emerging Atlantic slave trade took full advantage of the situation, and a number of Gypsies were deported by the British, where they were sold to slave colonies in the West Indies and the New World. The logic for this manoeuvre was "to free the kingdom of the burden of many strong and idle beggars, Egyptians, common and notorious thieves, and other dissolute and loose persons banished and stigmatized for gross crimes"[40].

With that all said, it's quite easy to understand why any GRT pupils in your class with some ancestral awareness (and they probably have) might not enjoy the lesson quite as much as their peers. This lack of connection or the unintentional isolation caused by such topics can result in what may appear to be troublesome behaviour, a lack of interest, or poor performance on tests and examinations. Remember, revered figures in the 'settled' world may in fact be despised persons in the GRT world. Such people – including Henry VIII, could be, as the Romani Gypsy academic Ian Hancock proposes, 'the same person who once sent our people to their deaths, or had Romani

---

[40] Goring, R. (2008).

families broken apart and imprisoned or shipped overseas'[41].

On the flipside, *positive* influence does not always arrive from the most likely of sources, nor does it always hold the same shared values that those in non-GRT communities may assume all to adhere to. During a period of my research I was investigating how marriage was understood and treated within particular communities. I was interested in the religious and theological narrative, and in finding its origins and systems of support. From personal experience I was aware of many apparent elements of difference (or alternative values and perspectives) between that of the 'settled' populous and the Gypsy and Traveller community. The most apparent being the age in which one chooses to marry.

For example, over the past 50 years British culture has gradually moved away from younger people (under 20 years of age) marrying. Whereas getting married at 17 or 18 years of age was once a commonality, the average age for marriage in the UK now stands at 37.5 years for men, and 35.1 years for women. However, getting married as young as 16 or 17 years of age in Gypsy and Traveller communities is still relatively common place.

---

[41] Hancock, I. (2013).

As a father of daughters, I was unfortunately more than aware of my girls' understandings regarding marriage (rolls eyes). After walking into their rooms on multiple occasions and witnessing yet another marriage between Prince Charming and whatever lucky doll had been selected that day, it was clear that they had marriage as thought process somewhere in their grey matter. The continual drawing of wedding dresses by one of them confirmed this fact. They like many young people around the world had gained an understanding of marriage not just from seeing parents and relatives, but also through well-known animated films that depicted Princesses. I was therefore not surprised to see the same phenomenon when conducting the aforementioned field research.

However, I was surprised at the consistent degree to which these films, their messages (both explicit and implicit) and their images were seemingly adopted by many young Gypsy and Traveller girls. Unhelpful television programmes that have been alluded to within this book had clearly picked up on this theme, and had made a point by placing a focus on a minor narrative at play, namely the design of their wedding dresses. However, whilst I am certain this element holds great value (I can feel my girls burning holes in my head with their eyes), it was secondary to the intrinsic values and beliefs that were being readily digested and adopted by the children.

For example, many of these 'Princesses' displayed certain moral codes and behaviours that were being exercised amongst some of those whom I interviewed. The mothers of the girls told me how it was 'proper' for their daughters to avoid cutting their hair shorter until they were married, how their daughters should be chaperoned when mixing with the opposite sex, and that to get married was both something to look forward to and an honourable thing. These approaches were a stark reminder that of all the well-known Princesses, there was only one who had shorter hair, and she lived with seven (small) men! Whilst being a humorous example, it is also an effective explanation behind many different unspoken narratives that are at play amongst some young GRT girls.

Once again, as we saw in the opening of this chapter, storytelling merges with real life to explain history, patterns of practice within the culture, and inherent beliefs. They become cultural parables, explaining one's own situation through the analogy of another. In this way, they are not fabricated tales, mere folklore, or simply fond memories. But storytelling in this regard is an important and significant method of communication. As a non-GRT person, understanding this concept should increase your awareness of the significance of communicating effectively, clearly and inclusively to your Gypsy and Traveller pupils. One method to achieve this is to simply look a little further into narratives that may hold a different value for others when planning lessons. By asking exploratory questions, you can quickly discover what themes or lessons may require a slight reworking or extra explanation. Whilst this will not happen often, you may find that the lessons most effected will be centred on subjects dealing with history, relationships, sex education, and certain religious festivals. For many new teachers / educators, approaching these areas with parents and pupils is sometimes a difficult process. Concerns over causing potential offence and potentially acting upon assumptions and/or stereotypes are among some of the reasons I have heard as to why said teachers do not always engage fully. The following two chapters will provide some assistance in both the practicalities of engagement, and in addressing said potential stereotypes.

CHAPTER FIVE: Building a Relationship with the Student and Parents

When I was studying for my PhD, I encountered many challenges. One of the greatest challenges that a researcher conducting ethnographic investigations encounters (particularly with GRT communities), is getting close to and within the environment of those being studied. For me, it was a familiar environment that I had spent a great deal of time in, where a number of friends and family resided. My thesis, which focused heavily on Gypsy and Traveller beliefs and practices required a huge degree of intimacy and trust with those whom I spoke to and interviewed. For the 'regular' ethnographer, developing these relationships is key in the process of obtaining the data needed. However, I – like many other researchers who had decided to research Traveller and Gypsy culture, encountered a particular 'invisible barrier' that worked to prevent the research getting 'too deep'.

As teachers, lecturers, pastoral support staff, social workers and many other roles, a key to being successful in teaching, reaching, and helping your GRT students, pupils and clients, is to build solid bridges of trust. My research would never have gotten off the ground, or gone to the depths that it reached, had it not been for the efforts made to build genuine and open relationships with the Gypsies and Travellers that I worked with.

Now for some – particularly school teachers, time is a factor in this process; limited one-on-one pupil time, coupled with the fact that Travellers sometimes do just as the name implies – travel, means that a quality relationship just simply doesn't materialise. This is because our usual notion of a quality and trusting relationship is one that is often built around the idea of time. For example, a good and strong marriage is never associated with those on their honeymoon, but for those who whose marriage has 'stood the test of time'. Such couples have seemingly been together forever, and it is this length of time that ultimately is indicative of the quality of their marriage. But this is merely an illusion; old married couples have had more arguments than newer couples. Furthermore, many 'older couples' are engaging in divorce proceedings than ever before. Age it would seem, provides experience – it does not necessarily provide happiness (or in our situation – results)!

The lack of time available to us as professionals with our GRT students and clients does not mean that an immovable barrier has been raised. It simply means that we have to be like the couple on the honeymoon: open; direct; trusting; mutually respectful; ignorant to the minor grievances; and only seeing the good in the other person.

First Things First

Some Traveller and Gypsy communities can appear structured and ordered; not necessarily in a 'hierarchical' sense (although sometimes this is the case), but in a generational sense. This means that there is a great deal of respect and honour for relatives that have passed away, or for ancestors who accomplished great things, or even for relatives that may be well known. This tier of respect, is then micronized, and is present within the home setting too. Dad may be head of the household, but it is mum that is sending him out to work. So a GRT family may initially have all the hallmarks of a patriarchal system, but in fact is closer to a matriarchy instead. This doesn't negate that areas of inequality may exist within some GRT communities. But it does mean that in order to begin to reach out, we must first put aside our own particular values, and allow ourselves to see the world through someone else's eyes; patriarchy for Travellers and Gypsies is not quite the demon that it is in the modern West.

Part of the purpose of knowing this structural perception, is that it gives us a clue as to who we must first engage, in order to reach our intended person. More often than not, securing a good relationship with the parents is the first step in reaching the pupil. By ensuring that a good working relationship with the parents is maintained, you will reap more benefits than simply being able to reach your pupils. Once word has spread that you are a 'good teacher' that doesn't judge but fights for the Gypsies' corner, then you will often find that you will become a beacon to which other Gypsy and Traveller parents will go to. I have seen schools attract additional good, hardworking GRT children committed to staying in school, all from word-of-mouth, because of an honest teacher, who is supportive of their children. Approaching Gypsy and Traveller parents should be done in just the same way as you would with any other parents. But you may have to instigate conversation and dialogue with the parents first.

What follows next is a checklist of pointers on how (and how not) to instigate these interactions, based on cultural differences in language, beliefs, and values. It is not definitive, in that there are of course many different *individuals* in the GRT *community*, but it is based on collective research and understandings of GRT societies. It is important to remember, and it goes without saying, that one should never act or respond to others, based on known stereotypes or prejudices. The following list may appear to enforce or (conversely) breakdown these stereotypes that you may know or even hold. It may be that you are a Gypsy or Traveller yourself, and that you wholeheartedly disagree with what is said. However, the information contained therein, is representative of a researched *majority* of Travellers and Gypsies; it could never fully encapsulate everyone and their individual thoughts and perceptions. As such, this list should serve as a helpful assistant. But it is important that you deal with every GRT individual as that – an individual. Hopefully the following information will assist in that process:

1 – *Be direct*. If you want to speak to the parents, avoid being overtly and unnaturally 'polite' and coy. Get to the point, and then gradually develop small talk. This may feel counter-intuitive, as conventionally in British culture, small talk comes first. Being direct shows confidence and honesty; there may be an element of mistrust, which will only be exaggerated if you begin with a 'how's the weather' conversation, only to inform the parents that little Billy has been reprimanded all week. Remember, any mistrust towards you is because of the 'badge' you wear, your position, what you potentially represent, and the values that you may be influencing their child with. It is not a personal mistrust, but being indirect and misleading could turn it into a personal issue.

2 – *Be yourself*. There's nothing worse than being something that you are not. Tying in with the previous point, not being genuine to who you are is a sure-fire way to developing mistrust in your relationship with the parent. This includes aspects of cultural appropriation, which I have witnessed countless times between non-Travellers and GRT people. So often during interviews or lectures that I have conducted, I am met by at least one or two comments of 'my (*insert relatives name here) is/was a Traveller', or 'I've got Gypsy blood in my family'. It gets even worse when I hear professionals attempting to relate to their GRT client in this way. It becomes a form of disingenuous empathy that is more cringe-worthy than commendable. I wouldn't run a clinic for deaf people, only to tell each person there that I once lost my hearing during an ear infection, or that my grandad was deaf; it means nothing and contributes even less. Perhaps when you've got to really know them, that introducing these details may help, but until that stage, don't authenticate your position and undermine their cultural heritage by telling them about your spurious links to Gypsy society.

3 – *Check your language*. You may have a 1st from Oxford, you may be a Countdown champion, and you may even be the human Google (my nickname, by the way). But don't let your knowledge get in the way of your accessibility. The combination of knowledge and a decent education has the wonderful consequence of an increased vocabulary, which in turn often allows for an exuberant array of oral expression (in other words, you can talk and write nicely). But complicating your language, or using overtly academic terminology in both your speech, letters you send home and your reports, can sometimes be seen as an air of superiority, or arrogance. Drop the fancy talk and be 'real'. Again, be direct (*see point one*). Importantly, don't mistake this need to simplify your language as an indicator of the Traveller parent's intellect; there are considerably more educated and informed Gypsies than you can imagine, and the historical cultural shunning of a traditional education system is not necessarily conterminous with being intellectually challenged.

4 – *Read between the lines*. I apologise for using a phrase to begin this point with, but it really is necessary. In a way, this is almost a 'point 3 – part 2', as it continues with the theme of language. This time however, it is the language of the parent. For the most part, there shouldn't be any language barriers or challenges to understanding. But there are a few things to be aware of when speaking to some Gypsy parents. Firstly, it's okay to admit that you haven't understood everything that has been said. Guy Ritchie's comedy thriller 'Snatch' (2000) played upon the stereotype of language issues amongst Irish Travellers and their English counterparts. Brad Pitt plays the role of 'Mickey' – an Irish Traveller boxing champion, who causes some of his fellow characters, namely 'Turkish' (played by Jason Statham), no end of difficulties, as Turkish and his sidekick Tommy constantly struggle to understand what is being said by Mickey. Whilst Snatch is arguably quite offensive to some, it highlights a valid point, that as people groups and differing cultures, we all have different accents and dialects. If you happen to mishear or misunderstand what the parents have said, treat it exactly how you would with any person who you misheard – ask them to repeat it!

Keeping on the theme of language, bear in mind that approaches to language may differ as well. I once watched a sporting event with a German friend (no, it wasn't football), and his favourite driver performed a great manoeuvre. To the untrained ear. It sounded like he was fuming, but in reality, he was extremely happy. Our cultural differences meant that our expressions were vastly different. Whilst it is by no means representative of all or even the majority of Travellers, it can be said that sometimes the language may be 'harsh' or seem threatening. To many Gypsies, the thought that their speech may be portraying them as aggressive would be horrifying. Please bear that in mind.

5 – *Get to know them*. Once you have begun regular interaction with your GRT parents and students, begin to progress the relationship further. Some pointers for conversation: Never disclose information about finances – money being earnt and money being spent; money can be a private subject in Traveller circles and you should respect it as such. As you would with any person, avoid using unsavoury or cursing language; the majority of Gypsies and Travellers identify as Christian, and the misuse of your speech could be seen as an indicator of your character. Avoid sexual referencing or sexualised comments, for the same reason as the misuse of language. Ask about where they live, and be genuinely interested – not concerned or judgemental, but interested. Get them to introduce you to other GRT parents at the school, and treat them exactly the same. And finally, see them for who they are, and not for what you think they may be.

By working with the parents, you are gradually able to develop a shared sense of value concerning the education that you and your school / institution are providing. For a long time there was a cultural trend, whereby progression beyond Primary school for many GRT people was not traditionally seen as necessary. Education at a Primary level provided the basics, whilst the awaiting world of work for the up-and-coming teenager was to provide the *real* education.

This cultural trend began changing during the 1970's, where newly emerging legislation meant that many trades had to be supported by official documentation and/or qualifications. The seemingly 'forced' assimilation naturally created some resistance, and to a certain degree still does. A number of GRT parents currently opt to home-school their children, understanding the necessity for a traditional academic education, but doing so under their terms. Unfortunately some schools in the UK, recognising the damaging effect to Ofsted ratings caused by low attendance, have actively encouraged their GRT families and other families fitting the criteria to educate from home!

However, many GRT families are fully engaged within mainstream education. Their only barrier often being the prejudices that those standing in front of them hold. But still, for some in the GRT community, the change is too fast and not to be trusted; for many others, the changes couldn't come fast enough.

As a teacher, a lecturer, a pastoral carer – you have to be prepared for a variety of attitudes and hugely varying abilities. Within these positions you are invaluably placed to bring about massive positive social change; not to dismiss any cultural values, but to ensure that Traveller and Gypsy culture transitions successfully into the next phase of its existence. The trickle-effect of developing these relationships is not to be underestimated. You will be contributing to the support and development of an underrepresented and marginalised community. You will be installing confidence in a people group that has historically shunned conventional education. And you will be developing bridges of social cohesion between two cultures that have a great deal of misunderstanding between them.

Visible Differences – Invisible Recognition

By getting the parents on-side, you may have gone some way in securing the efforts of your GRT pupils. But for arguments sake, let's assume that you have minimal or no contact with the parents at all – it's just you and the children. So how and why may the GRT pupils in your care be any different to any of the other children around them? For starters, they probably won't be any different; they will share the same interests and concerns as their peers. I can assure you that there is no difference between a Gypsy child playing with an XBOX or PlayStation, and a non-Gypsy child doing the same! However, there will be occasions where social values and norms play a part, and where there may be confusions in what is acceptable and what is not. For now, it is a case of understanding your position in relation to the pupil.

In many ways, you should begin by re-examining the previous five points on getting to know the parents. These same steps can be adapted and instigated in much the same way, taking into account the difference in nature of typical conversation. However, getting to know your pupils a lot more quickly is key…

So, with the previous list in mind, below is an extension of what is essentially a two-step process of getting to know your GRT community – parents first, children second:

1 – *Maintain authority.* Teaching approaches in the classroom have and continue to change, as new approaches replace seemingly outdated ideas on the correct way to direct the classroom, only to be replaced with an older model again at some point in the future. Age-old adages such as the instruction to not smile before the end of the first term continue to form part of the unofficial advice given to student teachers embarking on their teaching careers. Whilst some of these ideas remain relevant, it is always important to remember the teacher-student dynamic. With regards to 'traditional' Gypsy and Traveller students however, there are a few adaptions necessary, in order to remain 'in control'; this is not because GRT pupils have some odd genetic disposition to disrupt and be inattentive, but because of the social conditioning that may have happened for them beyond the school gates.

In the early stages of getting to know your pupils, it may be tempting to be extra friendly to those whom may appear to be disruptive; this a normal reaction but not always a helpful one. You are an alleged figure of authority; you need to, at least in the first instance, convey this position to the pupil. Be nice of course, but maybe take it easy on the comedy front. Several years ago, I was working as a TA in a Primary school with a significant 'pupil premium' and 'SEN' demographic. There was a continual tension between the 'class clowns' and one or two 'tough guys' in the class. I spent time getting to know the angry and at times violent young men, only to discover that they were both Travellers. They revealed to me how they didn't respect people acting like fools, and that they shared this same disrespect for their teacher – who would occasionally laugh at the funny kids' behaviour. In classes I've led, the Gypsy and Traveller children have shown an amazing sense of humour, and can often be the life of the class. However, they didn't – as the old saying goes, suffer fools gladly.

2 – *Don't treat Gypsies and Travellers differently*. Okay, so this might sound like a massive contradiction, but stick with it. Yes there are some massive cultural differences, but these children are desperate to fit in and not necessarily be noticed. When or if you respond to GRT pupils differently to other pupils, it should be at most subtle, and on a one-on-one basis – not in front of the whole class. It is not a one rule for one, and one rule for another. It is a fine line, but you will figure it out as you get to know the Travellers and Gypsies in your care / community.

Gypsy and Traveller children often suffer horrendous bullying, in all stages of education and beyond. They will rarely if ever report it, and will sooner disappear than 'lose face' by admitting to something potentially perceived as a weakness. By highlighting any particular differences in a public manner, you may inadvertently be contributing to that child's bullying or isolation. There are positive ways that you can support the cultural elements of your GRT pupils. Several schools and institutions now include amongst their diversity teaching, Gypsy and Traveller history days or weeks, where GRT heritage is celebrated. This provides a safe space in which the GRT pupils feel secure and celebrated, knowing that their peers are welcoming towards them and interested in their differences. Consider encouraging your GRT pupils to get involved, not forgetting to tell their parents how well they have represented their community at school!

I recently conducted research at a Secondary school in England, where the pupils told me that they felt safe and confident, simply because their teachers treated them no differently to any other pupils. Some had attended other schools previously, who they felt had been severe with them owing to their ethnic identity. A report produced in early 2016 that was later discussed in a roundtable event in the Houses of Parliament, reported that GRT pupils were 27 times more likely to be excluded from school than their non-GRT peers.

3 – *Celebrate the rewards*. Everything in Gypsy and Traveller culture is done with intent, effort, and purpose. If someone is going to work, then it is to get an income; if someone is going to school, then there needs to be a purpose – a conclusion as such. Simply informing the pupil that by learning 'X' will mean that they will get a good grade in the upcoming test is not good enough. They will want to know why and for what purpose getting a good grade will achieve. Will it mean that there will be a tangible reward at the end? Will it mean that they will be one step closer to earning a good wage? These are real rewards with real incentives. Be creative with this process but realistic. And when they work hard for you (and they will), then be sure to celebrate their successes with their parents as well.

4 – *Watch that language*. It seems sad to have to mention language as an element, but I have encountered many teachers who have questioned the nature of the language used by a number of their GRT pupils. The problem however is sometimes more to do with a subconscious focus leaning towards seeking out poor behaviour or *difference*. The fact that statistically GRT pupils are much more likely to be expelled or have sanctions placed against them at school could be used as evidence to dispute the subconscious factor. But in the same respect, if we aware that a Gypsy or Traveller is at greater risk of expulsion, we are more likely to recognise, be drawn to, and respond to the negative behaviour over any positives. This exposes a degree of accountability on our behalf – the professional. As such, we must look towards *our* response and behaviour towards that child if such a statistic is to change.

Without wanting to sound like a broken record, Gypsy and Traveller children are no different to any other children. I have had several teachers in the past speak to me about their 'Gypsy and Traveller' pupils, only to discover that they weren't Gypsies or Travellers at all, with one student teacher asking me '*but aren't they the same as chavs*'? I have no idea if that particular teacher ever qualified! Thankfully that is an extremely rare example, but it highlights an uncomfortable stereotype. The example given was drawn from conversations about the use of language by pupils. Several teachers had noted that their (confirmed) GRT pupils often used coarse language or vulgar terms, almost as a part of their regular language. They were unsure as to how to challenge this, without causing further issues in their classes.

Whilst an overwhelming majority of GRT pupils will be respectful, with their language following suit, there will be – as with any collection of pupils regardless of background, a certain element that use foul language. This has often been cited as one of the contributory reasons behind dismissals from school, as the pupil consistently engaged in antisocial and disruptive behaviour. Bad language amongst pupils is usually challenged by teachers, and it should continue to be done this way. However, when your GRT pupils are addressing you directly, if their language appears to be threatening or inappropriate, try to avoid taking it personally. It almost never is intended in a truly insulting way, but as a way of testing and establishing relational boundaries with you – the authority. They are not intending on breaking the rules, but seeing where they reside. For those who are parents, you will recognise this dynamic with your own children, as they apparently 'rebel' at varying stages. The 'terrible twos' is swiftly followed by a progression of anti-parent behaviour around the age of six to seven, and again around 13. If you are at the receiving end of inappropriate language, then persevere, as you are closer to a breakthrough than you realise.

Summary

There are many other points that could be added to this list, but these require greater explanation and timing, and as such, they are strategically placed throughout this book. In the meantime, these approaches should provide you with a solid foundation in which you begin to reach and teach GRT people within your establishment. To summarise, with both parents and pupils it is important to maintain a consistent level of respect from the outset. Transparency and trueness to oneself is key. Don't be afraid to ask questions; the worst that can happen is that you have to apologise to someone. Be interested and be curious; being seen as a person and as a contact for GRT parents and pupils in your schools and other places can have incredibly powerful effects on class productivity and institutional respectability. And above all, remember that your GRT pupils are human beings and individuals before they are anything else; treat them accordingly and you will be well on your way to forging successful relationships.

Developing these skills and the confidence to apply them usually rests in having some form of prior knowledge. Hopefully the previous chapters have gone some way in delivering this knowledge. However, I have found that in almost all of my workshops that I have delivered to teachers and professionals, that this development in awareness often leads to many more questions than it does answers! Curiosity, a new-found fascination, and a genuine desire to create inclusive environments with fellow citizens who happen to have an incredible heritage and culture, all come together in a barrage of questions. It's at that point that people usually feel comfortable in addressing queries that they believe may be based on stereotypes and/or potentially ethnically offensive beliefs. This almost always results in extremely positive conversation, with teachers, tutors and lecturers feeling inspired to be as supportive and encouraging as possible to their GRT pupils and students. As such, the following chapter will recreate elements of some of my workshops, by addressing common questions and stereotypes surrounding GRT communities and people.

CHAPTER SIX: Common Questions, Stereotypes, Terms and Definitions

All of the questions included in this chapter are taken from real life workshops that I have conducted. They were asked by educators and professionals (health care, local government, etc.) of varying experience (i.e. new or trainee teachers, experienced managers). Some of the questions revolved around the usage or meaning behind certain words and/or terms. In these instances, I have opted to simply include them within a 'terms and definitions' format, for ease of use and access. Furthermore, to assist in locating answers to particular themes, the questions have been grouped into sections of a similar nature. Finally, some of the questions are paraphrased to ensure clarity and conciseness.

It's important to remember that the questions and answers are not 'complete' per se, with many deserving far greater explanation and discussion. Of equal importance is to remember that whilst this chapter (and indeed, this book) serves as a convenient method of easy-access data, that Gypsy, Traveller and Roma communities are comprised of individuals. And as such, every person holds particular 'truths'; in short, our views on life, on our life, and on the lives around us, are subjective. Therefore, the information contained herein should serve as a guide, rather than as concrete terms and answers.

Common Questions and Stereotypes

Clothing and Appearance

A lot of the Travellers that I know wear large amounts of gold jewellery; the ladies seem to have those creole earrings, and the men have big rings, sometimes chains too. Is this a cultural thing (or even a thing at all)?

There is some truth behind this stereotype, although it does appear to be changing and it isn't just Travellers – it can include Gypsies and Roma people also. The situation started (and continues to some degree) due to a combination of social factors. One explanation is that for many years (centuries), many GRT people either couldn't access normal services (such as Banks) or simply didn't trust authorities to look after and manage their finances. This meant that their wealth had to stay with them. Keeping money on oneself is risky, and can also lead to a devaluation of funds – i.e. over time, money gradually becomes worth less. By investing in gold, the money was both secure – because it was always attached someway to the owner, and it was always worth something – as gold generally holds its price or gets more valuable with time. Having gold on display has also been used as a method of displaying how wealthy a person is, although this element is not exclusive to Gypsies or Travellers in any way. As the majority of Gypsies and Travellers live in fixed accommodation, the trend to invest in and wear gold is a matter of personal choice and not a cultural practice.

Do Gypsy and Traveller brides wear big, outlandish and sometimes colourful wedding dresses?

For the most part, no! Certain programmes on British and American television channels have shown brides and bridesmaids, as well as young girls on their Catholic Baptisms wearing such attire. But as with the general population, this is both very limited and a matter of personal choice and taste. It is not distinctly 'Gypsy' to wear an enormous dress, nor is it 'Gypsy' to wear a small dress; it's a matter of one's own taste.

The Gypsies (men) who live close to our house seem to wear a lot of 'country' style clothing – tweed, green or hunting style jackets, 'old men' flat caps, chequered shirts and Chelsea boots. Do a lot of Gypsies dress like this, and if so, why?

Gypsies and Travellers in the UK have been known for horse breeding and selling, and often living in the countryside, or at least on the margins of towns and cities. There are elements of truth within all of these factors. As such, there are a number of Gypsy and Traveller men who may dress this way because of where they live. However, for the most part this has been out of necessity, and is therefore no different to the tastes and requirements of any of the non-GRT people who live in such areas or who work in similar areas and trades. There may be a factor of 'group affiliation', whereby choosing to wear a certain style may indicate an immediate association to a certain group. This of course is a global phenomenon that can witnessed in almost every walk of life. However, to associate this as a definitive trend amongst GRT people in the UK without proper research would be improper.

I thought that Travellers were not allowed to have sex or proper relationships before marriage. So why do they all wear short dresses and hot pants on TV?

There is a lot to unpack in this question. For details concerning sex and relationship ideas, see the section, '*Relationships, Sexuality, and Gender Difference*'. For now, we will start with answering the primary assumption within the question. Not all Travellers (girls) wear short dresses and hot pants! A lot of the time, Gypsy and Traveller girls (minors) will choose and wear their clothing based on the same 'rules' that any other girl from any other social, ethnic, or racial group will adhere to: What do I like to wear? Will my parents allow me to wear it? What is the occasion? Sensationalised television programmes often only represent extremes of the focus group in question. As you can see from the questions in this section, such programmes have a lot to answer for.

Nomadicy and Settled Living

Do all Gypsies and Travellers live in caravans?

No. In fact, the vast majority of GRT people live in fixed accommodation. Such accommodation is mostly made up of 'bricks and mortar' – i.e. houses, flats, bungalows etc. However, 'fixed' can also include static caravans that are permanently fixed on legal sites. Some GRT people live a full or partial nomadic life, having no fixed location for their place of accommodation. A small minority are unable to secure fixed accommodation or permanent pitches on sites. This minority of technically 'homeless' GRT people are often those who many non-GRT people wrongly assume to be representative of most Gypsies and Travellers.

This stereotype mostly originates from certain 'romanticised' descriptions and stories of Gypsies that originated in the very late nineteenth and early twentieth century. These stories focused on the 'traditional' canvas and wooden-topped vardos (caravans) that could be seen travelling up and down country lanes. Interestingly, the idea of Gypsies always being nomadic and living in caravans didn't start until around this period, mostly owing to the fact that caravans in the sense that we understand them didn't exist until this time. Most UK Gypsies before this were settled, with the primary time of being a 'nomadic people' being the diaspora through Europe some four to five hundred years previous.

Why do Travellers always leave lots of rubbish behind when they leave somewhere?

Statistically Travellers or Gypsies who leave an illegal or non-registered stopping place, such as a public park, a lay-by or car park for example, are more likely to take their waste / rubbish with them. However, owing to a number of circumstances, there is a percentage who do leave rubbish behind, but it is vitally important to understand how and why this occasionally happens.

To begin with, as mentioned in the previous question, the percentage of Gypsies and Travellers who are permanently nomadic is very low. Out of this percentage, a small minority may leave behind waste. The primary reason for left waste in this situation is the lack of waste management provision by local authorities – i.e. bins and rubbish collection. It's easy to suggest that the Gypsies or Travellers in question take the rubbish with them, but where are they to dispose of the rubbish? In a bid to reduce fly-tipping[42], many local Councils and authorities refuse to let people driving vans and larger vehicles without specialist permits to get rid of their waste at 'rubbish tips'. Most nomadic GRT people drive such vehicles in order to be able to transport their caravans and to facilitate their business and employment. As such, they are not able to effectively get rid of their waste either at tips or designated facilities.

Relationships, Sexuality, and Gender Differences

On a TV programme I saw, the women stayed at home and were cleaning all day and/or looking after lots of children. Are women subservient to men in Gypsy communities, and are they allowed to work outside of the home?

To answer this, we need to look at the question in two parts. Firstly, many Gypsies and Travellers are both proud of their homes and of their personal presentation. Keeping one's home clean and spotless is therefore an essential extension of the upkeep of one's personal image. There is of course a practical element to this, and that is health and hygiene. This is more vital when travelling. Gypsies and

---

[42] 'Fly-tipping is a criminal offence in the UK. It involves dumping rubbish or waste of any kind (household, work-related) in places not designated or permitted for such purposes, like country lanes and car parks.

Travellers who live in this manner will often keep their homes clean to an incredible extent.

Social expectations and roles for many years meant that this upkeep of home and supervision of children was undertaken almost exclusively by females – girls and women. But this is no different to how the rest of the UK – and indeed many other western countries conducted themselves for centuries. However, it is a misconception to assume that some form of patriarchy is in operation. From personal experience it is quite the opposite! Females are often 'in charge' in more than a few capacities. In these situations it was a case of rather than the woman being forced to stay at home, it was the man having to go out to work and get an income for the wife and family.

Much like other countries and communities, this trend as well as many others in the GRT community is changing, albeit quite slowly in comparison to the larger populous. There are many successful female Gypsies and Travellers who have their own businesses and/or work in a variety of positions, including influential posts such as lawyers and academics. In separate research, I interviewed some GRT pupils at a Secondary school. They were all ambitious (males and females), and had plans for further education, and all had firm ideas about what they were planning to do career-wise. The females were interested in Law, running a beauty salon, and getting into senior retail management.

These realities were a far cry from the male-dominated images depicted in many forms of popular media.

I heard that Gypsies and Travellers aren't allowed to have sex before marriage. Is this true?

To some extent (and in an ideal world), yes. However, this has been part of a communal identity that has found its roots within religious foundations – Christianity for the most part, but also elements of Hinduism, and in some parts of Eastern Europe, Islam. Such an identity has been built around traditional conservative ideas that propose sex before marriage is immoral, spiritually wrong and Biblically impermissible.

Marriage is often held in high regard within many GRT circles, with 'divorce' being a dirty word and an often unentertained concept. As such, maintaining sexual 'purity' is for many GRT people an important element of cultural identity. However, this is an 'ideal' and as such there is little in the way that anyone can effectively police such an area or accurately report on it either. Therefore it's impossible to say how much truth there is in the actual practice of the statement, but that such a statement has at times been rightfully associated with a large amount of GRT people. Humans are human and have always had sex! But sometimes the idea of holding onto an idealistic value is what is important to people. In this instance, maintaining some form of purity that a lot of people outside of the community don't adhere to, is one of many methods of cultural preservation.

Language

What does the term 'Pikey' mean? Is it actually offensive? And is it used by Gypsies and Travellers?

The term 'Pikey' is an extremely offensive term to any GRT person. It comes from the Old English term 'Pikka', meaning to pick, pickpocket and/or steal. From the 16/17th century, 'Pikey' became a derogatory slur for those considered to be 'less than', 'criminal', and 'deviant'. Certain vagrancy acts meant that Gypsies were classified within these same terms, along with homeless people and other 'undesirable' people. At some point 'Pikey' became a term used exclusively to identify GRT people.

It should be considered to be as offensive as other well-known racist terms used to describe other races and ethnicities. I have never heard a Gypsy or Traveller use the term to describe or single out another GRT person. Worryingly, at the time of writing this, upon entering the word 'Pikey' into arguably the world's most famous internet search engine, the result provided is simply '*a Gypsy or Traveller*'! Give it a try now. This is an indication of the ingrained and uneducated narrative that has shaped many people's perspectives and understandings concerning GRT people.

I thought all Travellers were Irish. So why do some Travellers speak with an Irish accent, and others don't?

As this book has shown, there are some people within the collective GRT ethnicity who consider themselves to be Romani Gypsies, others who identify as Roma, and others who wish their ethnicity to be recorded as 'Traveller'. There are in fact many more collectives, names and terms around the world! Traveller ethnicity finds its genesis in Ireland – hence 'Irish Travellers'. There are around 31,000 Irish Travellers living in Ireland (around 4000 in Northern Ireland), and approximately 15–16,000 in the rest of the UK, hence why many Travellers speak in an Irish accent. Some Travellers have lived for generations in other areas or countries – including the USA, or have simply lived in various places for extended periods of time. This explains why a number of other Travellers speak with different accents.

Further to this, for a number of reasons some GRT people choose to be identified by particular names within the GRT spectrum that is different to their original identifier. For example, in some areas and in certain periods of history the term 'Gypsy' brought about negative connotations, and so the individual or family might have changed their ethnic identity from 'Gypsy' to 'Traveller', and vice versa.

> *There are two unrelated families of Gypsies in my school. They are lovely people but I sometimes have trouble understanding everything that they are saying. I feel rude to ask them to repeat themselves. Why is it sometimes difficult to understand some Gypsies?*

This is a common negative stereotype which highlights a natural prejudice that singles out Gypsies and Travellers. We'll look into that in a moment, but first let's look at the difficulty you are facing. There are three primary factors that contribute to some Gypsies and Travellers speaking in a way that others may find challenging to understand.

Firstly, a lot of GRT heritage is located in nomadic activity. This means that for generations, lots of GRT families would travel around; sometimes solely in the UK, and sometimes abroad as well. As with anyone else – GRT or not, certain accents, tones and words are picked up and 'adopted' by the listener. Gypsies and Travellers are no different to this natural rule. For example, my family are mostly from the South East of England, meaning that we all speak with a strong hint of London and Kent, with a bit of Essex thrown in for good measure! However, some of the words and terms we use are reflective of both my mother's upbringing and my family's Nordic heritage.

This leads us onto the second factor. Within many Gypsy and Traveller families (which can sometimes be very large and often very tight-knit), these terms, phrases and accents tend to be recycled and developed over the years. This results in conversations that are at times inaccessible to people outside of that loop. It's not an intentional exclusionary measure or anything out the ordinary; it's simply a phenomenon that can be witnessed in any group, amongst any people, anywhere in the world. However, this application of specific language however raises the third factor – Romani.

Romani is a language unique to GRT people the world over. However, there are, as with any other languages, many dialects, many names, and many variations. It isn't usually the primary language used by most GRT people, and some do not use it or know any terms at all. Certain Romani terms have unknowingly been adopted by the larger settled populous. Some of these terms are mentioned in the next main section, *'Common Terms and Definitions'*. So aside from the occasional application of Romani terms, these other factors for misunderstanding or not fully grasping the language used by a minority of GRT people, are actually common amongst every people group.

In short, it is not a problem unique to Gypsies and Travellers. Some time ago I was on holiday in a small village in Wales. I had great difficulty in understanding anything that was said, and I don't think the locals understood me either! However, it was not a 'Welsh' problem, nor was it an 'English' problem; in the same manner, Gypsy and Traveller dialect and language is not the problem either. Beyond this, there are some GRT academics who give specific attention to the fascinating area of Romani (and other Gypsy languages and dialects). If you're interested in this area, look out for work by the Gypsy scholar Ian Hancock, who has written extensively on this area.

Work and Trade

Is it true that lots of Gypsies and Travellers do tarmacking / building driveways for a living?

Historically many Gypsies and Travellers have been self-employed – partly out of necessity (i.e. discrimination in accessing certain jobs, positions and trades), but mostly out of personal choice. There is a rich tradition of passing down skills and trades to younger generations, which amongst males has typically included a lot of manual labour (including specialisms such as builders, landscape gardeners, carpenters and much more). For a long time many of these trades did not require qualifications or certifications, which resulted in a large number of GRT males dropping out of school during their teen years. As many trades are now requiring registration (for insurance and monitoring purposes), the trend for dropping out of school is rapidly declining. The decision to take children out of the schooling system should not be mistaken for a lack of interest in education by either the parents or the children.

Returning to the crux of the question, the answer is simply, no. There are a number of GRT people that will build driveways and tarmac areas for a living. But it is equally true that there are many more GRT people who work and operate in every area. There are successful property developers, lawyers, teachers, Police officers, beauticians, academics, cleaners, ministers, shop workers, musicians, footballers, and many, many more – all who are from Gypsy, Traveller or Roma families. Stereotypes limit our social narrative. If we allow such stereotypes to persist, then they can limit the social narrative of others too.

Animals

I've seen lots of pictures showing Travellers with horses; riding them, washing them in rivers, and pulling carts (traps). Are horses important to Travellers and Gypsies?

It's fair to say that many Gypsies and Travellers have had some encounter/s with horses, or may even be fortunate to even own one (or several). Horses have been an important and greatly loved animal to many GRT communities for many years and for many reasons. Whilst traditionally a working element within GRT life, horses have continued to play a significant role beyond cars and vans taking over the burden of transporting homes around the country and continent. Most serve as loved and prised possessions. There is a traditional horse trade within parts of the GRT community. This trade has been responsible for some of the historic and celebratory fairs and events that take place throughout the UK during the warmer months, including the world-famous 'Appleby Horse Fair'. There a number of Gypsies and Travellers who attend these events – not because they own horse, but because such events bring people, friends and families together. In this way, it could be said that the horse serves as a sort of symbol, displaying unity, collective identity and tradition.

When I was younger, I remember on occasions seeing small groups of Gypsies (my dad told me they were Gypsies) in the fields off the back from where I lived. They had dogs with them, and my dad said they would be hunting for Hares. Is there likely to be any truth in this? And if so, are there any other animals that Gypsies / Travellers use or hunt?

The activity your dad is talking about is 'Hare coursing'. Obviously it's impossible to say whether or not the people in question were Gypsies / Travellers. Hare coursing is a traditional hunting 'sport' that has been practised for many years by different people groups (settled, GRT, and more).

It involves using one or two dogs – often a Lurcher (a sturdy version of a Grey Hound), who is then sent after a Hare or rabbit. Sometimes bets can be placed on whether the Hare is caught or not, and sometimes it is purely a hunting event where the Hare or rabbit is used for food. As it is often illegal to conduct such activities (owing to land ownership), it's impossible to say how often such events may happen, and if Gypsies or Travellers are involved.

What is true is that many types of animal have historically been important and loved elements of Gypsy and Traveller life. Certain breeds of dog have traditionally been more popular than others, with Lurcher, Jack Russell and other Terrier varieties being prime choices. But as is highlighted with many of the other questions in this chapter, it all comes down to personal choice and preference. Suggesting an entire ethnic group conducts a certain activity, wears the same things, speaks the same way, or has the same values as each other is as foolish as it sounds.

However, we should not be afraid of asking questions. By doing so, we can understand both ourselves (including stereotypical attitudes and misinformed perspectives) and others (including specific cultural nuances, practices and qualities). One area we can do this is via conversation. The next section provides a brief extension of our discussion on language and communication by looking at a few familiar and common terms within GRT circles that you may have heard of or use.

Common Terms and Definitions

Many of the following terms are English Romani. Some Gypsies and Travellers will use these words and many others on a regular basis, whilst others will use certain terms at particular times. As Romani is a language in its own right, this list could be extensive. However, I have opted to simply include a few terms that you may have heard and are unsure as to what they mean, or may have assumed they had a different origin. There are a number of Romani academics who specialise in linguistics who expand upon this area in great volume and detail. If you have GRT pupils in your care who speak Romani, you should encourage them to continue speaking and learning in it, as it is both a fascinating and evolving language, and an important form of cultural identity.

Atchin – Stopping; Staying.

Bar – Pound (currency – British Sterling).

Chavy / Chavvie – A child.

Chore – Steal.

Chored / Chordi – Stolen.

Gypsies & Travellers: A Teacher's Guide

Diddakoi / Diddikai – Derogatory term meaning 'half-Gypsy' or 'half-blood', suggesting someone is not fully or proper Gypsy.

Drom – Road.

Gavvers – Police.

Gorger / Gorgies / Gadje / Gadzhe – Someone who isn't Gypsy, Traveller or Roma.

Kushti – Nice; Good; of a good standard; Approved.

Mokhhadi / Mokkadi – (Ritually) Unclean / (Ritually) Pure. A seemingly contradictory term that has evolved in meaning and which used properly has a great depth to its meaning.

Mush – A man. Sometimes used as a greeting; *'Alright mush, how are you?'*

Pani – Water.

Poggadi Jib – Meaning 'broken tongue' (with specific reference towards the amalgamated English–Romani language).

Tan – Home.

Trailer – A caravan or mobile home.

Vardo – *See 'Trailer'.

Wagon – *See 'Trailer'.

Concluding Remarks

To begin, the historical narrative in *Chapter One* has shown us that there are two sides to the GRT story – one of persecution and one of resilience. A thousand year story starting in India, followed by hundreds of years spent moving through Europe, has resulted in an ethnic minority that survived a diaspora, capital punishment, slavery and genocide. Fortunately the story never ended. Instead it produced chapters filled with new expressions of old religions, of languages formed from hundreds of tongues, and countless examples of ingenuity and tenacity.

We have seen how religion and spirituality has proved to be both persistent and pivotal in the development of Gypsy and Traveller identity, and how this has continued to translate into the contemporary period amongst the young and the old. Within the varying religious and social expressions of belief and practice are hints of a universal cultural identity, namely in the form of a belief that is focused on purity and preservational separateness from the outside world. These beliefs stretch back as far as the dawn of Roma inception, and continue to inform and direct the rationale of many Gypsies and Travellers the world over.

With this knowledge in hand, there comes an understanding that inclusivity (with a particular focus on GRT young people) must be pursued. *Chapter Five* showed that this can be partially accomplished by developing good relationships with parents. Good relationships in this context are constructed with honesty, trust, persistence and a sincere lack of prejudice. Further to this, understanding the differing nuances between settled and GRT cultures enables bridges to be built and relationships to grow.

The basis and nature of these relationships appear to be contradictory, in that they should be approached in the same way as you would with any other pupil, but with certain allowances for cultural differences. As highlighted, this is not covert language for preferential or different treatment. It is however a recommendation for *accommodating* treatment. As we are respectful and supportive of differing religions, sexualities, gender identities and other ethnic practices, so must the same accommodation be given to GRT people in our care. A simple method of finding out what these often personal needs and requirements are, is to simply ask those in your care. Another introductory method of course would be to give copies of this book to your colleagues! Either way, forming solid, trustworthy relationships with GRT people with whom you hold a responsibility for, should be undertaken in a nonbiased and accommodating fashion.

Accommodating others when their outlook on life is potentially vastly different from your own is not always easy or comfortable. Many Gypsy boys approaching adolescence will expect to be spoken and treated with the same respect as any adult – even if their behaviour (as any 12 year old boy would be) can be challenging at times. The same can be said for girls in your charge, who may be just a few short years away from becoming a wife and a mother. Some of these practices, beliefs, trends and cultural patterns are changing, evolving and some are even ending. But it is important to remember that as an educator within a professional setting, it is your role to educate, encourage and be there for that child and/or family. It is *not* your role to change or question the culture before you. However, asking questions *about* that culture based upon genuine objective enquiry is an entirely different thing altogether.

The same objectivity will prove to be invaluable when developing lessons, activities, homework, classroom displays, waiting areas and other environments. By first exploring (time permitting) the history and/or context of how you will fill these areas, you might just avoid unnecessary offence and upset. Examples alluded to st various junctures in this book, such as the Henry VIII account, expose potentially damaging aspects of our 'shared' history, whereby our particular ethnic and ancestral outcomes are not necessarily the same as the person we are sat next to. Indeed, even simple elements of daily life or conversation, such as small talk regarding relationships or how we dress, might be vastly different to the new Gypsy or Traveller family that have started attending your school or facility.

Of course, one of the most direct ways to avoiding these offences, to building relationships, to developing trust, and to providing authentic accommodation, is to lose our beliefs in certain stereotypes that we have bought into or allowed to continue unchallenged. This final chapter has provided a simple example of how open, direct and sometimes explicit conversation can open doors and break down barriers in an unflinching and non-compromised fashion. For if we are to genuinely abandon the harmful stereotypes that we believe to be correct, then we must first find out what is true and what is false, what is myth and what is factual.

In the meantime, take on board the message of inclusivity within this book. If you can apply it – great. If it needs modifying to the differing people in your care – modify it. But please don't allow another generation of young GRT people to be abandoned to the vicious teeth of prejudice and the insatiable appetite of discrimination. Famous artist (and not-so-famous Gypsy) Picasso once said, 'Action is the foundational key to all success'. With that said and done, the ball, as they say, is in your court. Kushti Bok! (Good luck).

BIBLIOGRAPHY

A Selection of Works Cited and/or Consulted:

Acton, T. (1974) *Gypsy Politics and Social Change: The Development of Ethnic Ideology and Pressure Politics among British Gypsies from Victorian Reformism to Romany Nationalism*. London: Routledge.

Acton, T. & Mundy, G. (1999) *Romani Culture and Gypsy Identity*. Hertfordshire: University of Hertfordshire Press.

Bhopal, K. (2006) 'Issues of Rurality and Good Practice: Gypsy Traveller Pupils in School', in Neal, S. & Agyeman, J. (Eds.) *The New Countryside? Ethnicity, Nation and Exclusion in Contemporary Rural Britain*. Bristol: Policy Press.

Bhopal, K. & Myers, M. (2008) *Insiders, Outsiders and Others: Gypsies and Identity*. Hatfield: University of Hertfordshire.

Cameron, J. (2014) *Racism and Hate: An American Reality*. Bloomington, IN: AuthorHouse LLC.

Clark, C. & Greenfields, M. (2006) *Here to Stay: The Gypsies and Travellers of Britain*. Hatfield: University of Hertfordshire Press.

Cribb, A. & Gewirtz, S. (2009) *Understanding Education: A Sociological Perspective.* Cambridge: Polity Press.

Cudworth, D. (2008) "There is a little bit more than just delivering the stuff': Policy, pedagogy and the education of Gypsy/Traveller children', in *Critical Social Policy*, Vol. 28, Issue 3, pp. 361-377.

Dawson, R. (2000) *Gypsy Codes and Taboo*. Derbyshire: Blackwell Publishing Ltd.

Dennis, N. (2001) *The Uncertain Trumpet: A History of Church of England School Education to AD 2001*. London: Civitas.

Duggan, C. (2006) 'Lombroso, Cesare (1835-1909)', in Claeys, G. (ed.) *Encyclopaedia of Nineteenth Century Thought*. Abingdon, Oxen: Routledge Ltd.

Fraser, A. (1995) *The Gypsies*. Oxford: Blackwell Publishing.

Goring, R. (2008) '*Scotland: An Autobiography: 2,000 Years of Scottish History by Those Who Saw it Happen*'. New York: The Overlook Press.

Hancock, I. (2000) 'Standardisation and Ethnic Defence in Emergent Non-Literate Societies: The Gypsy and Caribbean Cases', in Acton, T. & Dalphinis, M. (Eds.) *Language, Blacks and Gypsies*. London: Whiting and Birch.

Hancock, I. (2001) 'The Romani Element in Non-Standard Speech by Yaron Matras. Review by: Ian Hancock', in *Anthropological Linguistics*, Vol. 43, (No. 4), pp. 515 – 519.

Hancock, I. (2013) *We are the Romani People*. Hatfield: University of Hertfordshire Press.

Horne, S. (2014) *'What Travellers Believe and Why it Matters to the Church and Educational Providers'*, BA (Hons), Unpublished: Canterbury Christ Church University.

Horne, S. (In Press) 'Cerefino Giminéz Malla: Gypsy Saint – Christian Martyr', in Prentis, S. (Ed.) *Inspired Souls – Faith Stories of Black Saints and Holy People from Around the World*. London: Church House Publishing.

Keet-Black, J. (2013) *Gypsies of Britain*. Oxford: Shire Publications Ltd.

Le Bas, D. & Acton, T. (2010) *All Change! Romani Studies through Romani Eyes: The Possible Implications of Diasporic Consciousness for Romani Identity*. Hatfield: University of Hertfordshire Press.

Le Bas, D. (2018) *The Stopping Places: A Journey Through Gypsy Britain*. London: Chatto and Windus.

Lee, R. (2001) 'The Rom-Vlach Gypsies and the Kris-Romani', in Weyrauch, W. (Ed.) *Gypsy Law: Romani Legal Traditions and Culture*. London: University of California Press.

Moore, G. (2004) *Nietzsche, Biology and Metaphor*. Cambridge: Cambridge University Press.

Muncey, T. (2010) *Creating Autoethnographies*. London: SAGE Publications.

Okely, J (1998) *The Traveller-Gypsies*. Cambridge: Cambridge University Press.

Raines, J. (2002) *Marx on Religion.* Philadelphia: Temple University Press.

Rapport, F., Wainwright, P., & Elwyn, G. (2005) 'Of the Edgelands: Broadening the Scope of Qualitative Methodology', in *Medical Humanities*, Vol. 31 (No. 1), pp. 37 – 43.

Reilly, K., Kaufman, S. & Bodino, A. (2003) *Racism: A Global Reader.* New York: M. E. Sharpe, Inc.

Shoard, M. (2002) 'Edgelands', in Jenkins, J. (Ed.) *Remaking the Landscape: The Changing Face of Britain.* London: Profile Books.

Stewart, M. (1997) *The Time of the Gypsies.* Oxford: Westview Press.
Taylor, B. (2008) *A Minority and the State: Travellers in Britain in the Twentieth Century.* Manchester: Manchester University Press.

Taylor, B. (2014) *Another Darkness, Another Dawn: A History of Gypsies, Roma and Travellers.* London: Reaktion Books Ltd.

Wells, D. (1907) 'Social Darwinism', in *American Journal of Sociology*, Vol. 12 (No. 5) (March 1907), pp. 695 – 716.

Weyrauch, W. (2001) *Gypsy Law: Romani Legal Traditions and Culture.* London: University of California Press Ltd.

Gypsies & Travellers: A Teacher's Guide

Steven Horne

ABOUT THE AUTHOR

Steven Horne is a University Lecturer in Primary Education, Theology, and Religious Studies, and the founder of 'The Gypsy Education Network'. Alongside other positions, during the past 20 years Steven has worked with and taught young people and marginalised groups in various settings and countries. This has shaped and informed his research, writing and activism, which for the past decade has almost exclusively focused on GRT communities and issues. Steven's research (soon to be published) extensively covers Gypsy and Traveller beliefs, belief systems, spiritualism, theology, and associated practices.

Copyright © 2019 Steven Horne. All rights reserved.

Printed in Great Britain
by Amazon